slow
cooking

from around the mediterranean

carolyn humphries

foulsham
LONDON • NEW YORK • TORONTO • SYDNEY

foulsham

The Publishing House, Bennetts Close, Cippenham, Slough,
Berkshire, SL1 5AP, England

Foulsham books can be found in all good bookshops and direct from
www.foulsham.com

ISBN: 978–0–572–03323–1

Copyright © 2007 W. Foulsham & Co. Ltd

Cover photograph © The Anthony Blake Picture Library

A CIP record for this book is available from the British Library

The moral right of the author has been asserted

Other books for your slow cooker:
Slow Cooking from Around the World (978-0-572-03289-0)
New Recipes for Your Slo-cooker (978-0-572-02636-3)
Real Food from Your Slo-cooker (978-0-572-02536-6)
Slow Cooking for Yourself (978-0-572-03150-3)

Printed in Great Britain by Mackays Ltd, Chatham, Kent

CONTENTS

INTRODUCTION

Mediterranean food is, arguably, among the most well known and popular in the world. The glorious fruits, such as citrus, peaches, nectarines, melons, tomatoes, figs and olives; the stunningly colourful vegetables, such as aubergines (eggplants), artichokes, (bell) peppers, courgettes (zucchini), garlic and onions; the fragrant herbs and spices; the rustic dried beans, breads, cured meats and sausages; the magnificent seafood; the abundant array of cheeses from cows, sheep, goats and buffalo; and, of course, the fabulous wines to wash it all down with.

Whether you are cooking hearty dishes like my version of *bollito* – an Italian peasant speciality of a selection of meats and vegetables gently braised for hours until meltingly tender – or more elegant fare such as the classic *coq au vin* – chicken cooked in white burgundy with button (pearl) onions and mushrooms – you will find your slow cooker invaluable for making great Mediterranean food.

But don't think you can cook only soups and stews! You can create wonderful pâtés and fish, vegetable, pasta and rice dishes as well as a range of undeniably exquisite desserts. This book is packed with modern Mediterranean food at its best, from all the countries that border the ocean – France, Italy, Spain, Portugal, Morocco, Turkey and Greece – and all the recipes can be made in a simple, leisurely way in your slow cooker.

USING YOUR SLOW COOKER

1 Stand the electric base on a level, heat-resistant surface. Do not use on the floor.

2 Do not preheat your pot unless your manufacturer's instructions tell you to.

3 Put the ingredients in the ceramic crock pot, then put the pot in the base.

4 Add boiling liquid.

5 Cover with the lid and select the cooking temperature (High, Medium or Low).

6 Cook for the recommended time, checking after the shorter time if a range is given. This will usually be sufficient for most cookers but the food won't spoil if it is cooked for the extra time.

7 Taste, stir and re-season, if necessary.

8 Switch off the cooker and remove the crock pot using oven gloves.

COOKING TIPS FOR USING THE SLOW COOKER

- Any of your usual soup, stew or casserole recipes can be cooked in your slow cooker but liquid doesn't evaporate as much as it does when cooking conventionally, so cut down the liquid content by 30–50 per cent (not quite so important for soups) or increase the flour or cornflour (cornstarch) thickener by one-third. You can always add a little extra liquid at the end of cooking, if necessary.
- Should there be too much liquid at the end of cooking, strain it into a saucepan and boil rapidly for several minutes until reduced to the quantity you require, or thicken it with a little flour or cornflour blended with a little water.
- If wanting a brown finish to meat or poultry, fry it quickly in a frying pan before adding to the crock pot.
- For many dishes, it is best to quickly fry onions before adding them – the flavour is completely different from slow-cooking them from raw.
- Make sure all frozen foods are thawed before use.
- Cut root vegetables into small, even-sized pieces and put them towards the bottom of the pot as they will take longer than meat or other vegetables to cook.
- Do not cook too large a joint or bird in the crock pot. It should fit in the pot with at least a 2.5 cm/1 in headspace. If unsure, cut the joint or bird in half before cooking (it will then cook quicker, as when cooking conventionally).
- Most foods can be slow-cooked but pasta (unless pre-cooked) and seafood should be added for the last hour, and cream at the end of cooking. All the recipes in this book tell you how and when to do this.
- Dried beans must be boiled rapidly in a saucepan of water for at least 10 minutes before adding them to your crock pot, to destroy toxins.

- If preparing food the night before you wish to start cooking, store the ingredients in the fridge overnight. Put them in the crock pot in the morning and cover with boiling liquid or sauce before cooking.
- Do not open the lid unnecessarily during cooking as heat will be lost. If you remove it to add extra ingredients or to stir more than once or twice, you may need to add on an extra 10 minutes at the end (but in most cases there is sufficient cooking time built in to allow for this).
- When cooking soups, make sure there is a 5 cm/2 in headspace in the pot to allow for bubbling during cooking.
- When food is cooked, the cooker can be switched off and left for up to 30 minutes. The food will stay piping hot. If you need to leave food keeping hot for longer, switch to Low.
- If you are unsure if a joint of meat or a bird is cooked through, check by inserting a meat thermometer at the end of cooking.
- Most foods can be cooked on High or Low (or Medium or Auto-cook if you have them). Fish, rice and egg-based dishes, however, must be cooked on Low.
- If you are planning on being out all day, opt for cooking on Low, then there is little or no chance of the meal spoiling even if you are late (particularly if you don't have a programmable slow cooker).
- You can use the crock pot to keep hot drinks such as mulled wine warm, or for hot dips or fondues. Keep the pot on the Low setting.
- Use a crock pot suitable for the quantity of food you want to cook. It should be at least a third to half full for best results, though for foods like ribs or chicken wings a single layer in a large pot is fine. Don't use a small pot and pack it tightly to the top or the heat won't be able to penetrate the food – just as when cooking conventionally. But, conversely, don't have too little either. For instance, one chop in the pot will overcook unless the pot is at least filled up to a third with liquid. So, if cooking for one, you may need to double the amount of liquid to be on the safe side.

LOOKING AFTER YOUR SLOW COOKER

- Do not put the crock pot or the lid in the oven, freezer or microwave, or on the hob, or under the grill (broiler).
- Do not plunge the hot pot into cold water after cooking or it may crack.
- Do not leave the whole pot soaking in water as the base is unglazed and porous so will absorb the water. You may, however, leave water *in* the pot to soak it before washing.
- Do not preheat the cooker before adding the ingredients (unless your manufacturer's instructions tell you to).
- Do not use the slow cooker to reheat food.
- Do not leave uncooked food in the slow cooker when it is not switched on (so never put it in there overnight ready to switch on in the morning. Store the ingredients in the fridge).
- Do not use abrasive cleaners on the crock pot – but it will be dishwasher safe.
- Do not immerse the electric base in water; simply unplug it and wipe it clean with a damp cloth.

COOKING TIMES

Some crock pots now have three cooking settings but others have only two. I have cooked most foods on High or Low as they will be relevant to all. Use Medium or Low for any of them, if you prefer, and adjust the times according to the chart below.

Some cookers also have Auto-cook. Follow your manufacturer's guidelines to use it. I recommend you use Low if you are going to be out all day.

This chart also shows you the approximate conversion times from conventionally cooked soups, stews and casseroles, should you want to try your own recipes (but remember to reduce the liquid by at least a third). Always check your manufacturer's instructions too as their times may vary slightly.

The more you use your slow cooker, the more you will become used to the correct times for your own model.

Conventional cooking time	Slow cooking time in hours		
	High	Medium	Low
15–30 minutes	1–2	2–3	4–6
30 minutes–1 hour	2–3	3–4	5–7
1–2 hours	3–4	4–6	6–8
2–4 hours	5–6	6–8	8–12

NOTES ON THE RECIPES

- I designed these recipes, for the most part, to be cooked in a large oval 6.5 litre slow cooker but almost all can be cooked in a smaller round 3.5 litre cooker. Remember that some small models cook quite quickly on High, so you may prefer the Low setting.
- All ingredients are given in imperial, metric and American measures. Follow one set only in a recipe. American terms are given in brackets.
- The ingredients are listed in the order in which they are used in the recipe.
- All spoon measures are level: 1 tsp = 5 ml; 1 tbsp = 15 ml.
- Eggs are medium unless otherwise stated.
- Always wash, peel, core and seed, if necessary, fresh produce before use.
- Seasoning is very much a matter of personal taste. Taste the food before serving and adjust to suit your own palate.
- Fresh herbs are great for garnishing and adding flavour. Pots of them are available in all good supermarkets. Keep your favourite ones on the window sill and water them regularly. Jars of ready-prepared herbs, such as coriander (cilantro), and frozen ones – chopped parsley in particular – are also very useful. Don't use dried for garnishing.
- I have called for chopped fresh tomatoes rather than canned most of the time but you can always use canned instead if you prefer. On average, 4 tomatoes (or 2 beefsteak) will be the equivalent of a 400 g/14 oz/large can.
- When I call for stock, use fresh if possible, or make up the equivalent with stock cubes or powder.
- All can and packet sizes are approximate as they vary from brand to brand.

SOUPS

Well, they are ideal to make in a slow cooker, aren't they? Delicious bowlfuls of colourful concoctions, slowly cooked to perfection with no fuss, no steam and hardly any effort! Some need a little preparation – chopping, grating or pre-frying – but, once the ingredients are in the cooker, they can be left to do their own thing with little or no moisture loss so there's no need to worry that they'll boil dry. Throughout the Mediterranean there are loads of different soups that celebrate the best of its produce – vegetables, dried beans and lentils, meat, fish and poultry. Many of these soups provide pretty substantial fare that, with a few hunks of lovely fresh bread, make a meal in themselves.

Fish soups are popular throughout the Mediterranean. They would usually be made using the heads and bones from the seafood to make stock before making the final dish. But for the slow cooker it would defeat the object to do that first, so I've cheated and used ready-made stock. The red pepper and garlic rouille adds an exciting finish.

hearty fish soup with red pepper and garlic rouille

SERVES 4–6

FOR THE SOUP:
45 ml/3 tbsp olive oil
1 onion, finely chopped
2 garlic cloves, crushed
1 celery stick, finely chopped
1 carrot, finely chopped
2 beefsteak tomatoes, skinned and finely chopped
200 g/7 oz raw mixed seafood, thawed if frozen
225 g/8 oz monkfish or thick cod fillet, diced
150 g/5 oz tuna steak, diced
10 ml/2 tsp anchovy essence (extract)

15 ml/1 tbsp tomato purée (paste)
200 ml/7 fl oz/scant 1 cup dry white wine or cider
500 ml/17 fl oz/2¼ cups fish or chicken stock
1 bay leaf
Salt and freshly ground black pepper
15 ml/1 tbsp chopped fresh parsley

FOR THE ROUILLE:
1 red (bell) pepper
1 garlic clove, crushed
120 ml/4 fl oz/½ cup mayonnaise
15 ml/1 tbsp olive oil
Salt and freshly ground black pepper
A few drops of lemon juice

1 To make the soup, heat the oil in a frying pan, add the onion, garlic, celery and carrot and fry gently, stirring, for 3 minutes until softened but not browned. Tip into the crock pot.

2 Add the tomatoes and all the fish.

3 Put the anchovy essence, tomato purée, wine, stock and bay leaf in the frying pan. Bring to the boil, stirring, then tip into the pot. Cover and cook on Low for 4–5 hours.

4 Meanwhile, to make the rouille, roast the pepper under a preheated grill (broiler), turning occasionally, until blackened all over. Place in a plastic bag. When cool enough to handle, rub off the skin. Halve the pepper and remove the stalk and seeds.

5 Place the pepper in a blender with the garlic and blend until smooth, stopping and scraping down the sides as necessary. Add the mayonnaise and oil and blend again. Season to taste and sharpen with lemon juice. Tip into a small bowl and chill until ready to serve.

6 When the soup is cooked, discard the bay leaf and season to taste. Ladle into warm bowls, sprinkle with the parsley and serve with the rouille handed separately for each person to stir a large spoonful into their soup.

This glorious fresh version of the hearty Italian bean and vegetable soup is made with the best of the green vegetables and herbs of the area. Serve it with plenty of crusty bread and freshly grated Parmesan to sprinkle over for a nourishing light lunch or supper dish. You can keep a block of Parmesan in the fridge, which is more flavoursome than using ready grated.

green minestrone
with fresh basil

SERVES 6

1 bunch of spring onions (scallions), chopped
1 garlic clove, crushed
1 green (bell) pepper, finely chopped
1 courgette (zucchini), finely chopped
100 g/4 oz French (green) beans, finely chopped
1 small head of cavolo nero cabbage, finely shredded
300 g/11 oz/medium can of flageolet beans, drained

750 ml/1¼ pints/3 cups boiling vegetable or chicken stock
1 bay leaf
15 ml/1 tbsp olive oil
Salt and freshly ground black pepper
30 ml/2 tbsp chopped fresh basil
Freshly grated Parmesan cheese, to garnish

TO SERVE:
Crusty bread

1 Place all the ingredients except the salt, pepper and basil in the crock pot and stir well. Cover and cook on High for 3–4 hours until everything is tender.

2 Season to taste, discard the bay leaf and stir in the basil.

3 Ladle into warm bowls and sprinkle liberally with grated Parmesan before serving with crusty bread.

This is an Italian speciality from Tuscany. The poached eggs are not traditional but they do add a fantastic finishing touch. It makes a really substantial soup for a nourishing lunch or supper, or you can serve it in smaller portions as a starter before a simple salad or some bread and cheese. If you prefer, use a can of beans instead of fresh, and go from Step 2.

white bean and tomato soup with fennel and quails' eggs

SERVES 4

100 g/4 oz/⅔ cup dried haricot (navy) beans, soaked in cold water for several hours or overnight
15 ml/1 tbsp olive oil
1 large onion, finely chopped
1 garlic clove, crushed
1 head of fennel, finely chopped
4 beefsteak tomatoes, skinned and chopped
600 ml/1 pint/2½ cups boiling vegetable or chicken stock
90 ml/6 tbsp dry white wine

15 ml/1 tbsp tomato purée (paste)
5 ml/1 tsp light brown sugar
10 ml/2 tsp chopped fresh sage
10 ml/2 tsp chopped fresh thyme
Salt and freshly ground black pepper
8 quails' eggs
4 or 8 fresh sage leaves, to garnish

TO SERVE:
Warm ciabatta bread

1 Drain the beans and place in a saucepan. Cover with fresh water and boil rapidly for 10 minutes to remove toxins. Tip into the slow cooker, cover and cook on High for 3–4 hours until tender.

2 Meanwhile, heat the oil in a frying pan. Add the onion, garlic and fennel and fry gently for 2 minutes, stirring, until softened but not browned.

3 Tip into the beans and add all the remaining ingredients except the eggs. Re-cover and cook on High for 3 hours until everything is tender. Stir well, taste and re-season if necessary.

4 Carefully break the eggs into the soup. Cover and cook for a further 2–4 minutes or until they are cooked to your liking. Ladle into warm bowls, making sure everyone gets two eggs. Garnish each serving with one or two fresh sage leaves and serve with warm ciabatta bread.

This soup is often made with just lamb stock and rice and finished with the egg and lemon. Here there are chunky pieces of meat and vegetable in the soup, which makes it a satisfying meal rather than just a starter. Serving it with the buttery garlic pittas rounds it off perfectly. You can use a meaty roast lamb bone instead of the raw meat if you prefer.

greek lamb, courgette, egg and lemon soup with garlic pittas

SERVES 4–6

FOR THE SOUP:
½ small shoulder of lamb, trimmed
    of excess fat
1 onion, finely chopped
1.2 litres/2 pints/5 cups boiling
    water
1 bay leaf
5 ml/1 tsp salt
Freshly ground black pepper
2 courgettes (zucchini), diced

50 g/2 oz/¼ cup long-grain rice
Juice of 1 lemon
2 eggs, beaten

FOR THE PITTAS:
40 g/1½ oz/3 tbsp butter, softened
1 garlic clove, crushed
30 ml/2 tbsp chopped fresh parsley,
    plus extra for garnishing
Salt and freshly ground black pepper
4 pitta breads

1 To make the soup, put the lamb in the crock pot with the onion, water, bay leaf, salt and a good grinding of pepper. Cover and cook on High for 4–5 hours until the meat is very tender.

2 Add the courgettes, rice and lemon juice. Stir well, re-cover and cook on High for 1 hour until everything is soft. If necessary, skim off any fat from the surface.

3 To make the pittas, about 10 minutes before the soup will be ready mash the butter with the garlic and parsley and a little salt and pepper. Spread over one side of each pitta. Lay the breads on foil on the grill (broiler) rack. Cook under a preheated grill for about 2 minutes until hot through and the butter has melted. Turn off the grill, wrap up the breads in the foil so they absorb the melted butter and keep warm under the grill.

4 Lift the lamb out of the soup, remove the meat and discard the bones. Cut the meat into small pieces and return it to the soup. Turn off the slow cooker.

5 Whisk 2 ladlefuls of the stock into the beaten eggs, then stir back into the pot. Taste and re-season, if necessary.

6 Cut the pitta breads into fingers and place in a serving basket. Ladle the soup into large warm bowls, sprinkle with the parsley and serve with the garlic pittas.

This is harira, *the national soup of Morocco. Traditionally it is served during Ramadan to break the fast at sundown, and almost every household will prepare its own version. Some people use lamb instead of chicken and rice instead of pasta. Others use different legumes, such as brown lentils or butter beans.*

chicken and legume soup
with harissa

SERVES 4–6

75 g/3 oz/½ cup dried chick peas
(garbanzos), soaked in cold water
for several hours or overnight
2 chicken portions
50 g/2 oz/¼ cup red lentils
1 large onion, chopped
1 garlic clove, crushed
A pinch of saffron strands
15 ml/1 tbsp paprika
5 ml/1 tsp ground coriander
(cilantro)
5 ml/1 tsp ground cumin
5 ml/1 tsp salt

Freshly ground black pepper
400 g/14 oz/large can of chopped
tomatoes
15 ml/1 tbsp tomato purée (paste)
900 ml/1½ pints/3¾ cups boiling
chicken stock
15 ml/1 tbsp harissa paste
50 g/2 oz vermicelli, broken into
short lengths
A handful of chopped fresh
coriander and 1 thinly sliced
lemon, to garnish

1 Drain the chick peas, place in a saucepan and cover with fresh water. Bring to the boil and boil rapidly for 10 minutes, then reduce the heat and simmer for 45 minutes until almost tender. Drain and tip into the crock pot.

2 Add all the remaining ingredients except the harissa paste and vermicelli. Cover and cook on High for 3–4 hours.

3 Remove the chicken and stir the harissa paste and vermicelli into the soup. Re-cover and cook for a further 1 hour until everything is tender.

4 Meanwhile, take all the chicken off the bones and discard the skin. Cut the meat into small pieces. When the soup is cooked, stir in the chicken, taste and re-season, if necessary. Heat through for a further 5 minutes. Ladle into warm bowls, sprinkle with the coriander and add a slice or two of lemon to each bowl.

This classic from France, vichysoisse, *is delicious hot or chilled. I've added some peas to the mixture to give it added sweetness and a lovely green colour. Remember to turn down the slow cooker to Low before enriching the soup with the egg yolk and cream at the end of cooking, as it will curdle if it is allowed to boil.*

creamy leek and potato soup with croûtons

SERVES 6

FOR THE SOUP:
25 g/1 oz/2 tbsp butter
15 ml/1 tbsp sunflower oil
1 onion, finely chopped
2 large leeks, trimmed and sliced
2 large potatoes, peeled and diced
100 g/4 oz/1 cup frozen peas, thawed
750 ml/1¼ pints/3 cups boiling chicken or vegetable stock
1 bouquet garni sachet

Salt and freshly ground black pepper
150 ml/¼ pint/⅔ cup single (light) cream, plus a little extra for garnishing
1 egg yolk

FOR THE CROÛTONS:
30 ml/2 tbsp sunflower oil
25 g/1 oz/2 tbsp butter
2 slices of bread, cut into small cubes

1 To make the soup, heat the butter and oil in a saucepan. Add the onion and leeks and cook for 2 minutes, stirring, until softened but not browned.

2 Tip into the crock pot and add all the remaining ingredients except the cream and egg yolk. Cover and cook on High for 3–4 hours until really tender.

3 Discard the bouquet garni and transfer the soup to a blender or food processor. Purée until smooth. Add the cream and egg yolk and blend again. Taste and re-season, if necessary. Turn the slow cooker to Low and return the soup to the pot to reheat very gently.

4 Meanwhile, to make the croûtons, heat the oil and butter in a frying pan. Add the bread cubes and fry over a moderate heat, stirring, until golden all over. Drain on kitchen paper (paper towels).

5 Ladle the soup into warm bowls, add a swirl of cream to each and sprinkle with a few croûtons before serving.

French onion soup is a classic. Here I've used sweet red onions, cooked in the pot in a little butter and sugar first to soften and caramelise them, and then added the stock and slow cooked them to impart a wonderful rich flavour. The soup is then topped off with toasted slices of French bread smothered in sweet-cured ham and melting cheese.

caramelised french red onion soup with gruyère and ham croûtes

SERVES 4

25 g/1 oz/2 tbsp butter, cut into small flakes
4 large red onions, halved and thinly sliced
15 ml/1 tbsp light brown sugar
750 ml/1¼ pints/3 cups boiling beef stock

Salt and freshly ground black pepper
4 diagonally cut slices of French bread
2 slices of sweet-cured ham
50 g/2 oz/½ cup grated Gruyère (Swiss) cheese

1 Put the butter in the crock pot on High, cover and leave for about 15 minutes until melted. Add the onions and sugar, toss well, cover and cook for 2–3 hours until soft and turning lightly golden.

2 Add the stock and a little salt and pepper, re-cover and cook for a further 1–2 hours. Taste and re-season, if necessary.

3 Meanwhile, make the croûtes. Toast the bread on both sides under the grill (broiler). Add the ham, trimming it to fit, then pile the cheese on top. When ready to serve, toast again until the cheese melts and bubbles. Immediately ladle the soup into bowls, top each with a croûte and serve straight away.

This is really a thinned-down houmous! It makes a filling and really tasty soup, particularly if served with several colourful accompaniments to sprinkle into it before eating. I also like to serve it with lemon wedges to squeeze over, and warm pitta breads to accompany. Use a drained can of chick peas, if you like, and start at Step 2.

chick pea, tahini and red pepper soup

SERVES 4

100 g/4 oz/⅔ cup dried chick peas (garbanzos), soaked in cold water for several hours or overnight
30 ml/2 tbsp olive oil, plus extra for serving
1 large onion, chopped
1 large carrot, chopped
2 garlic cloves, crushed
2 red (bell) peppers, trimmed, cored and diced
5 ml/1 tsp ground cumin
5 ml/1 tsp ground turmeric
2.5 ml/½ tsp ground ginger
750 ml/1¼ pints/3 cups boiling vegetable stock

30 ml/2 tbsp tahini (sesame seed paste)
2.5 ml/½ tsp dried thyme
5 ml/1 tsp clear honey
1.5 ml/¼ tsp crushed dried chillies (optional)
Salt and freshly ground black pepper

FOR THE ACCOMPANIMENTS:
Small dishes of finely diced avocado, tossed in lemon juice, finely chopped tomato, sliced stoned (pitted) green and black olives, raisins

1 Drain the chick peas, place in a saucepan and cover with fresh water. Bring to the boil and boil rapidly for 15 minutes. Drain and tip into the crock pot.

2 Heat the oil in a frying pan, add the onion and carrot and fry for 2 minutes, stirring. Tip into the pot. Add all the remaining ingredients, cover and cook on High for 3–4 hours until the chick peas are really soft.

3 Purée the soup in a blender or food processor and return to the pot. Taste and re-season if necessary. Keep warm on Low until ready to serve.

4 Ladle into warm bowls, add a trickle of olive oil to each and serve with the dishes of accompaniments handed separately.

Variations of this soup are eaten all over Spain. They all contain either white or Savoy cabbage and chorizo sausage but some also have dried beans and others potato. I particularly like adding pimiento and a little hot pimentón to enhance the flavour, and to trickle extra virgin olive oil over before serving.

spicy sausage, cabbage and potato soup

SERVES 4

30 ml/2 tbsp olive oil, plus extra for
  serving
1 onion, chopped
1 large garlic clove, crushed
2.5 ml/½ tsp pimentón
100 g/4 oz piece of chorizo
  sausage, skinned and diced
2 large potatoes, diced
½ small white cabbage, chopped
2 pimiento caps, from a can or jar,
  drained and diced

5 ml/1 tsp chopped fresh rosemary
1.2 litres/2 pints/5 cups boiling
  chicken or vegetable stock
Salt and freshly ground black pepper
4 small sprigs of fresh rosemary
  (with flowers when in season), to
  garnish

TO SERVE:
Any rustic-style bread

1 Heat the oil in a frying pan, add the onion and garlic and fry gently, stirring, for 2 minutes. Tip into the crock pot.

2 Add all the remaining ingredients, cover and cook on High for 3–4 hours until the potatoes and cabbage are really tender.

3 Taste and re-season if necessary. Ladle into warm bowls, trickle a little olive oil over each and push a small sprig of rosemary into the soup at the edge of each bowl. Serve with rustic-style bread.

Even if you don't go mushroom picking, you can buy selections of different varieties in your local supermarket. They look wonderful and the flavour of this thin soup is second to none. When wild mushrooms are not in season, use cultivated open mushrooms instead. I use a food processor to finely chop the additional vegetables.

brandied wild mushroom soup with oregano cream

SERVES 4

15 g/½ oz/1 tbsp butter
30 ml/2 tbsp olive oil
1 onion, minced (ground) or finely chopped
1 large garlic clove, minced or finely chopped
1 carrot, minced or finely chopped
1 celery stick, minced or finely chopped
100 g/4 oz cultivated cup mushrooms, minced or finely chopped
750 ml/1¼ pints/3 cups chicken or vegetable stock
250 g/9 oz wild mushrooms, cut into neat pieces but not too small
10 ml/2 tsp mushroom ketchup (catsup)
30 ml/2 tbsp chopped fresh oregano
Salt and freshly ground black pepper
90 ml/6 tbsp crème fraîche
15 ml/1 tbsp chopped fresh parsley
30 ml/2 tbsp brandy

TO SERVE:
French bread

1 Heat the butter and half the oil in a saucepan, add the minced or chopped vegetables and fry gently, stirring, for 2 minutes until softened but not browned,

2 Add the stock, bring to the boil and tip into the crock pot.

3 Add the wild mushrooms, mushroom ketchup, half the oregano and a little salt and pepper. Cover and cook on High for 2–3 hours.

4 Meanwhile, mix the crème fraîche with the remaining oil and oregano and the parsley. Season to taste and chill until ready to serve.

5 When the soup is ready, stir in the brandy, taste and re-season if necessary. Ladle into large warm soup plates, top each with a spoonful of the oregano cream and serve with French bread.

This is based on a recipe I first enjoyed in Aix-en-Provence in the South of France. It is rich, sweet and beautifully golden. The watercress and lemon pistou adds colour, texture and a peppery sharpness. For a smoother consistency, use ground almonds instead of flaked. The pistou is also wonderful stirred through pasta with Parmesan shavings scattered over.

spiced sweet potato and pumpkin soup with watercress and lemon pistou

SERVES 6

FOR THE SOUP:
15 g/½ oz/1 tbsp butter
1 large onion, chopped
1 celery stick, chopped
½ small pumpkin, about 450 g/
    1 lb, seeded and diced
1 large sweet potato, diced
2.5 ml/½ tsp ground cumin
2.5 ml/½ tsp paprika
2.5 ml/½ tsp dried herbes de
    Provence

900 ml/1½ pints/3¾ cups boiling
    chicken or vegetable stock
Salt and freshly ground black pepper

FOR THE PISTOU:
1 bunch of watercress, stalks
    trimmed
50 g/2 oz/½ cup flaked (slivered)
    almonds
1 garlic clove, crushed
Grated zest of 1 lemon
5 ml/1 tsp lemon juice
90 ml/6 tbsp olive oil

1   To make the soup, heat the butter in a saucepan, add the onion and celery and fry, stirring, for 2 minutes until lightly golden. Add the pumpkin and sweet potato and toss to coat in the butter.

2   Tip into the crock pot and add all the remaining ingredients. Cover and cook on High for 3–4 hours until very tender.

3   Meanwhile, to make the pistou, put all the ingredients in a blender or food processor and run the machine until the mixture forms a coarse paste, stopping and scraping down the sides as necessary. Season to taste. Turn into a small bowl and chill until ready to serve.

4   When the soup is cooked, purée in a blender or food processor. Taste and re-season if necessary. Return to the crock pot on Low to keep warm until ready to serve ladled into warm soup bowls, with a spoonful of the pistou in each one.

This is a simple but fresh soup bursting with Mediterranean flavour.
Adding the spoonful of Mascarpone cheese is not traditional but it does
add an original enriching taste and texture. I like to serve it before a
prosciutto platter with olives, some melon, Mozzarella and more freshly
baked Italian ciabatta bread.

tomato and ciabatta bread soup with rocket and basil

SERVES 6

900 g/2 lb ripe plum tomatoes,
skinned and chopped
2 garlic cloves, crushed
1 bunch of spring onions (scallions),
finely chopped
10 ml/2 tsp clear honey
15 ml/1 tbsp white balsamic
condiment
250 ml/8 fl oz/1 cup boiling
vegetable stock

60 ml/4 tbsp dry vermouth
60 ml/4 tbsp olive oil
2 thick slices ciabatta bread, made
into breadcrumbs
25 g/1 oz wild rocket, chopped
15 ml/1 tbsp chopped fresh basil
60 ml/4 tbsp Mascarpone cheese
30 ml/2 tbsp milk
Salt and freshly ground black pepper
4 small basil leaves, to garnish

1   Put the tomatoes, garlic, spring onions, honey, balsamic condiment, stock, vermouth and oil in the crock pot. Cover and cook on High for 2–3 hours until the tomatoes are pulpy.

2   Stir in the breadcrumbs, rocket and basil and cook for a further 30 minutes.

3   Meanwhile, mix the Mascarpone with the milk to form a soft dropping consistency.

4   Season the soup to taste and ladle into warm open soup plates. Add a spoonful of the thinned Mascarpone to each and top each with a basil leaf.

STARTERS
AND
SNACKS

Obviously, many starters are cold salad creations that don't require cooking at all but there are numerous dishes that lend themselves perfectly to the slow cooker — pâtés and terrines, mousses and custards, dried bean dishes and anything else that would be gently cooked either on top of the stove or in the oven. The advantage with the slow cooker is that these dishes need little or no watching and timings are rarely crucial — except, perhaps, for egg-based, rice and pasta dishes. There are many Mediterranean specialities here, from French pork *rillettes* to the Italian *bagna cauda*.

Fonduta is a thick, creamy dish of cheese, milk, cream and eggs. The finished dish is slightly grainier than when cooked in a double saucepan but takes much less effort! You could use Cheddar, Edam or Gruyère cheese instead of Fontina, or a mixture of these. If you can, add some shavings of white truffle just before serving instead of the truffle oil.

piedmont fontina cheese dip with truffle oil

SERVES 4

20 ml/4 tsp cornflour (cornstarch)
150 ml/¼ pint/⅔ cup milk
2 large eggs
175 g/6 oz/1½ cups grated Fontina
   cheese
25 g/1 oz/2 tbsp unsalted (sweet)
   butter, cut into small flakes

Salt and freshly ground black pepper
90 ml/6 tbsp single (light) cream
5 ml/1 tsp truffle oil

TO SERVE:
Ciabatta bread, cut into small
   chunks

1 Whisk together the cornflour and milk in a small earthenware pot that will fit in the slow cooker. Whisk in the eggs.

2 Stir in the cheese and add the butter and some salt and pepper.

3 Stand the dish in the crock pot with enough boiling water to come half way up the side of the dish.

4 Cover and cook on Low for 2 hours or until thick, stirring well every 30 minutes.

5 Remove from the crock pot and beat well, then beat in the cream. Trickle the truffle oil over and serve straight away with small chunks of ciabatta bread for dunking.

This is the perfect terrine to serve for lunch with salad and crusty bread. I first had it in Marseilles in France many years ago. It is the ideal dish to cook in your slow cooker as it won't dry out but just becomes tender, rich and firm. Try it with a spoonful of cranberry sauce on the side or sliced apple tossed in lemon juice.

coarse pork terrine with pistachios

SERVES 8–10

12 rashers (slices) of streaky bacon, rinded
1 onion, quartered
2 garlic cloves, roughly chopped
6 sprigs of fresh parsley
450 g/1 lb belly pork, skinned
100 g/4 oz unsmoked bacon pieces, trimmed of any rind or gristle
350 g/12 oz pig's liver
5 ml/1 tsp dried herbes de Provence
1.5 ml/¼ tsp ground cloves
A good pinch of cayenne
30 ml/2 tbsp brandy
75 g/3 oz/¾ cup shelled pistachio nuts
7.5 ml/1½ tsp salt
Freshly ground black pepper

TO SERVE:
Crusty bread, mustard and a side salad

1   Line a 1.5 litre/2½ pint/6 cup terrine or large loaf tin with some of the bacon rashers, trimming to fit as necessary.

2   Using a food processor or mincer (grinder), process the onion, garlic, parsley, pork, bacon pieces and liver but not too finely.

3   Stir in the dried herbs, spices, brandy, pistachios, salt and a good grinding of pepper. Turn into the prepared terrine and level.

4   Top with the remaining bacon. Cover with greaseproof (waxed) paper, then a lid or foil, twisting and folding it under the rim to secure. Stand the terrine in the crock pot with enough boiling water to come half way up the sides of the terrine.

5   Cover and cook on High for 4–5 hours until firm to the touch and the juices are clear.

6   Remove from the crock pot and remove the cover. Top with some clean greaseproof paper and weigh down with heavy weights or cans of food. Leave until cold, then chill. If liked (particularly if using a loaf tin), loosen the edges and turn out on to a serving dish. Serve sliced with crusty bread, mustard and a side salad.

I've added sliced button mushrooms to a fairly smooth classic liver pâté to create this delicious recipe. It is very easy to prepare and makes a delicious starter or a light lunch with crusty bread and pickles. Cooking the mushrooms first in a little of the butter intensifies their flavour and eliminates some of their moisture.

chicken liver pâté with button mushrooms

SERVES 8–10

1 onion, peeled and quartered
2 garlic cloves, peeled and roughly chopped
450 g/1 lb chicken livers, trimmed
30 ml/2 tbsp brandy
2.5 ml/½ tsp dried mixed herbs
225 g/8 oz/1 cup butter, melted, plus a little extra for greasing
60 ml/4 tbsp double (heavy) cream

1 egg, beaten
Salt and freshly ground black pepper
175 g/6 oz button mushrooms, sliced
Mixed salad leaves and lemon wedges, to garnish

TO SERVE:
Toast

1 Place the onion, garlic, livers, brandy, herbs, about three-quarters of the butter, the cream and egg in a blender or food processor. Season generously and run the machine to make a smooth paste.

2 Put the remaining melted butter in a saucepan, add the mushrooms and fry, stirring, for 3 minutes until tender. Turn up the heat, if necessary to evaporate the liquid. Stir into the pâté mixture.

3 Grease a 1.5 litre/2½ pint/6 cup terrine or large loaf tin and line the base with non-stick baking parchment. Spoon the pâté into the tin and level the surface.

4 Cover with greaseproof (waxed) paper, then a lid or foil, twisting and folding under the rim to secure, and place in the crock pot with enough boiling water to come half way up the sides of the terrine. Cover and cook on High for 3–4 hours until firm to the touch.

5 Remove from the crock pot. Remove the lid or foil and re-cover with clean greaseproof paper. Leave to cool, then weigh down with heavy weights or cans of food and chill until firm.

6 Loosen the edge and turn out on to a board. Cut into thick slices and arrange on individual plates. Garnish each with a few salad leaves and a lemon wedge and serve with toast.

Rillettes is like a light and meaty pâté and is popular throughout France. If you enjoy it, it's worth making double the quantity I give here as it will keep for absolutely ages in the fridge. Serve it as a starter with toast or crusty bread or use it as a filling for baguettes, with some salad leaves and a touch of mustard.

potted pork with garlic and herbs

SERVES 4–6

500 g/18 oz fat belly pork
1 large garlic clove, crushed
7.5 ml/1½ tsp coarse sea salt
A sprig of fresh rosemary
1 bay leaf

1 clove
Freshly ground black pepper
45 ml/3 tbsp boiling water
25 g/1 oz/2 tbsp lard (shortening)

1   Cut off any bones and rind from the pork. Lay the meat in the crock pot with the bones and rind alongside. Add all the remaining ingredients except the lard, cover and cook on High for 5–6 hours.

2   Discard the herbs, clove, bones and rind. Tip the meat and juices into a sieve (strainer), cover and leave to drain and cool. Chill the liquid so the fat solidifies.

3   Tip the meat on to a board and, using two forks, shred the meat. Pack it into a clean jar.

4   Scoop the fat off the cooking juices and pour any juices below into the rillettes. Melt the fat with the lard and pour over the top of the meat. Seal the jar with a clean lid and store in the fridge for up to 1 month. Once the jar is opened, eat within 2 days.

For this recipe, I've blended the white beans with diced Parma ham,
olives, red onion and chopped fresh rosemary, all bathed in olive oil with a
dash of white balsamic condiment. If you prepare the salad ingredients
then leave the beans to cook in the crock pot, the dish can be thrown
together in minutes when you are ready to serve.

warm tuscan white
bean salad

SERVES 4–6

225 g/8 oz/1⅓ cup dried haricot
(navy) beans, soaked in cold
water for several hours or
overnight
1 litre/1¾ pints/4¼ cups boiling
water
4 slices of Parma (or similar raw)
ham, diced
50 g/2 oz/⅓ cup black olives
1 red onion, thinly sliced
2 sun-dried tomatoes, chopped

1 red (bell) pepper, chopped
10 ml/2 tsp chopped fresh rosemary
15 ml/1 tbsp chopped fresh basil
1 garlic clove, crushed
60 ml/4 tbsp olive oil
30 ml/2 tbsp white balsamic
condiment
Salt and freshly ground black pepper

TO SERVE:
Ciabatta bread

1 Drain the soaked beans and place in a saucepan with the boiling
water. Return to the boil and boil rapidly for 10 minutes.

2 Tip the beans and liquid into the crock pot, cover and cook on
High for 3–4 hours until the beans are really tender. If not ready to
eat, turn to Low.

3 When ready to serve, drain the beans in a colander and tip into a
large salad bowl. Add all the remaining ingredients and season
well. Toss well and serve while still warm with ciabatta bread.

Use large open cup mushrooms for this dish but don't choose ones that are too flat because the stuffing needs to sit in the cups. After the initial cooking on High, they can stay in the slow cooker for up to 2 hours on Low, but after that the texture becomes a little too soft. For added crunch, sprinkle the dish with some crisp crumbled bacon just before serving.

stuffed garlic mushrooms with cream and white wine

SERVES 4

8 large open cup mushrooms
75 g/3 oz/1½ cups soft breadcrumbs
2 spring onions (scallions), finely chopped
2 large garlic cloves, crushed
45 ml/3 tbsp chopped fresh parsley
Salt and freshly ground black pepper
1 egg, beaten

150 ml/¼ pint/⅔ cup dry white wine
8 tiny knobs of butter
150 ml/¼ pint/⅔ cup double (heavy) cream
4 small sprigs of fresh parsley, to garnish

TO SERVE:
Crusty bread

1 Peel the mushrooms and trim the stalks. Chop the stalks and mix with the breadcrumbs, spring onions, half the garlic and the parsley. Season well, then mix with the beaten egg.

2 Season the mushroom caps lightly, then press the stuffing mixture on to the gills of each one.

3 Pour the wine into the crock pot, add the remaining garlic and a little salt and pepper. Place the mushrooms on top, preferably in a single layer or just overlapping (if you have only a small round pot, put them in layers with baking parchment between the layers). Top each with a tiny knob of butter.

4 Cover and cook on High for 2–3 hours until the mushrooms are tender and the stuffing has set.

5 Transfer the mushrooms to warm small plates. Stir the cream into the wine juices, taste, re-season, if necessary, then spoon over. Garnish each plate with a small sprig of parsley and serve with crusty bread.

Bagna cauda is ideal for the slow cooker. It can stew very gently until the anchovies 'melt' into the oil. I add chopped rosemary and cream to the original mixture. Ideally, use a small slow cooker, otherwise put the mixture in a small round dish in a larger cooker with enough boiling water to come half way up the side of the dish.

italian melted anchovy dip

SERVES 4–6

2 × 50 g/2 oz/very small cans of anchovy fillets, drained, reserving the oil, and chopped
2 garlic cloves, crushed
100 g/4 oz/½ cup unsalted (sweet) butter, diced
15 ml/1 tbsp chopped fresh rosemary
90 ml/6 tbsp double (heavy) cream

FOR THE DIPPERS:
Cubes of focaccia or ciabatta bread, thick strips of red, yellow and green (bell) peppers, celery sticks cut into short lengths, sticks of raw carrot, sticks of cucumber

1 Put the anchovies, their oil, the garlic, butter and rosemary in the slow cooker. Cover and cook on High for 2–3 hours.

2 Stir well with a wire whisk to blend the anchovies into the oil and butter, then stir in the cream. Turn the heat to Low.

3 Ideally, place the slow cooker on the table and serve with the dippers, as you would for a fondue. Alternatively, pour the dip into warm small individual pots on plates and arrange the dippers around.

Avruga caviare is made from herring eggs and is so much better in texture and flavour than the Danish lumpfish roe. You can, however, substitute this cheaper alternative if you prefer. If you have only a small round slow cooker, make the mousse in a 15 cm/6 in soufflé dish and serve it in spoonfuls instead of turned out.

smoked salmon mousse
with avruga caviare

SERVES 6

175 g/6 oz smoked salmon
  trimmings
2 spring onions (scallions), roughly
  chopped
1 beefsteak tomato, skinned,
  quartered and seeded
450 ml/¾ pint/2 cups crème fraîche
Finely grated zest and juice of
  1 lemon
2 eggs, separated
Salt and freshly ground black pepper

Olive oil for greasing

FOR THE DRESSING:
90 ml/6 tbsp mayonnaise
30 ml/2 tbsp olive oil, plus extra for
  greasing
15 ml/1 tbsp chopped fresh parsley
15 ml/1 tbsp chopped fresh tarragon
55 g/2 oz/small jar of avruga caviare

TO SERVE:
Hot wholemeal toast

1 Drop the salmon, spring onions and tomato in a blender or food processor, a little at a time, with the machine running all the time. Stop and scrape down the sides as necessary. Alternatively, mince (grind) or very finely chop the ingredients (but this isn't so satisfactory).

2 Blend in the crème fraîche, 10 ml/2 tsp of the lemon juice, the egg yolks and salt and pepper to taste.

3 Whisk the egg whites until stiff, then fold into the salmon mixture with a metal spoon.

4 Grease six ramekins (custard cups) or dariole moulds with a little olive oil. Spoon the salmon mixture into the prepared dishes and cover each loosely with oiled foil. Stand them in the crock pot with enough boiling water to come half way up the sides of the dishes. Cover and cook on Low for 1½–2 hours until firm to the touch. Remove from the crock pot and leave to cool, then chill.

5 Meanwhile, to make the dressing, whisk together the mayonnaise, oil, herbs, the lemon zest and remaining lemon juice in a small bowl.

6 When ready to serve, gently loosen the edges of the mousses with a round-bladed knife and turn out on to the centres of six small plates. Top each with a spoonful of caviare. Spoon a trickle of the dressing around and serve immediately with hot wholemeal toast.

This is a classy way of serving Spain's favourite tapas. A tortilla is basically a potato omelette and you'd eat it in most Spanish households as well as in restaurants and bars. Here I've slow cooked the tortilla in the crock pot, then cut it into wedges and served it in a pool of spicy fresh tomato salsa.

spanish tortilla with piquant tomato salsa

SERVES 4 AS A LIGHT MEAL, 8 AS A TAPAS

FOR THE TORTILLA:
90 ml/6 tbsp olive oil
2 onions, thinly sliced
4 large potatoes, peeled and very
   thinly sliced (ideally using a
   mandolin)
6 eggs
Salt and freshly ground black pepper

FOR THE SALSA:
15 ml/1 tbsp olive oil
1 small onion, chopped
1 garlic clove, crushed
1.5 ml/¼ tsp crushed dried chillies
4 beefsteak tomatoes, skinned and
   chopped
60 ml/4 tbsp apple juice
2.5 ml/½ tsp dried oregano
30 ml/2 tbsp chopped fresh parsley

1   To make the tortilla, brush the crock pot with a little of the oil. Heat the remaining oil in a saucepan, add the onions and fry for 2 minutes, stirring.

2   Add the potatoes and toss well. Cook for a further 2 minutes, stirring, then tip the whole lot into the crock pot (keep the pan for making the salsa). Spread out the mixture as evenly as possible. Cover and cook on High for 1–2 hours until the potatoes are really tender.

3   Beat the eggs with some salt and pepper and pour into the pot. Stir well, then cover and cook for 30 minutes until set. (Note that the eggs are cooked on High, rather than on Low, to imitate frying).

4   Meanwhile, to make the salsa, heat the oil in the onion and potato saucepan. Add the onion and garlic and cook, stirring, for 2 minutes until they are softened but not browned.

5 Add all the remaining ingredients except the parsley. Bring to the boil and cook rapidly for 5 minutes until pulpy, stirring frequently. Transfer to a blender or food processor and blend to a purée. Taste and re-season if necessary, then return to the pan. Reheat when ready to serve.

6 When the tortilla is cooked, remove the crock pot from the base and leave the tortilla to cool for 5 minutes. Cut into wedges. Spoon the salsa on to warm plates and place one or two wedges of tortilla on top (if using two, put them at a jaunty angle one on top of the other). Sprinkle with the chopped parsley and serve.

These delicate parcels are called dolmades *in Greece, from where they originate. Although they are a bit fiddly to make, they are well worth it because the flavour is superb. Serve them as part of a mezze selection or salad plate, as finger food at parties – or just enjoy them as a tasty snack.*

vine leaves stuffed with rice, herbs, pine nuts and raisins

MAKES 24

50 g/2 oz/½ cup pine nuts
50 g/2 oz/⅓ cup raisins
100 g/4 oz/½ cup short grain
  (pudding) rice
1 garlic clove, crushed
1 small onion, finely chopped
5 ml/1 tsp dried oregano
5 ml/1 tsp dried mint
15 ml/1 tbsp tomato purée (paste)

2.5 ml/½ tsp salt
Freshly ground black pepper
2.5 ml/½ tsp ground cinnamon
24 vacuum-packed vine leaves,
  rinsed and dried
75 ml/5 tbsp olive oil
Juice of ½ lemon
About 750 ml/1¼ pints/3 cups
  boiling vegetable stock

1 Mix the pine nuts with the raisins, uncooked rice, garlic, onion, herbs, tomato purée, salt, lots of pepper and the cinnamon.

2 Put a small spoonful of the filling on each vine leaf, fold in the sides and roll up. Pack them tightly into the crock pot (this will take a while).

3 Add the oil and lemon juice, then pour over enough of the boiling stock to just cover the vine leaves. Cover and cook on High for 3 hours or until the rice is cooked and most of the liquid has been absorbed. Remove the crock pot from the base and leave the vine leaves to cool in the liquid.

4 Transfer the rolls to a serving platter with a draining spoon and serve at room temperature.

This is an exciting version of pickled herrings or mackerel, which are also popular in northern Europe. They are often rolled up around flavourings but here the mackerel is cooked over the flavourings in the oil and white wine, rather than the more usual vinegar, then served with some colourful sweet red peppers.

spanish mackerel with roasted red peppers

SERVES 4

1 large onion, halved and thinly sliced
2 celery sticks, cut into thin matchsticks
2 garlic cloves, finely chopped
2 cloves
2 bay leaves
4 small mackerel, filleted
150 ml/¼ pint/⅔ cup dry white wine

90 ml/6 tbsp olive oil, plus extra for drizzling
5 ml/1 tsp light brown sugar
Salt and freshly ground black pepper
4 red (bell) peppers
4 small fresh bay leaves, to garnish

TO SERVE:
Crusty bread

1 Spread out the onion and celery in the crock pot and sprinkle with the garlic. Add the cloves and bay leaves. Cut the mackerel fillets in halves lengthways and lay them on top, preferably in a single layer or, if not, divided by non-stick baking parchment.

2 Heat the wine, oil and sugar together with a little salt and pepper. Bring to the boil and pour over the mackerel.

3 Cover and cook on Low for 2 hours until the mackerel is tender. Remove the pot and leave to cool but do not chill.

4 Meanwhile, put the peppers under a preheated grill (broiler) and cook, turning occasionally, for about 15 minutes until the skin has blackened. Put the peppers in a plastic bag and, when cool enough to handle, rub off the skins. Discard the stalks and seeds, then cut the flesh into thin strips.

5 Lift the mackerel out of the cooking liquid and discard the cloves and bay leaves. Drain the onion and celery and arrange a small pile on each of four small plates. Top each with two mackerel fillets, then a small pile of red pepper strips. Drizzle a little olive oil over and around each plate, garnish each with a small bay leaf and serve with crusty bread.

This is the Egyptian speciality of beid hamine – slow-cooked eggs in onion skins to give the flesh a pale brown tinge and soft, creamy consistency. They are often served with ful medames – dried broad beans. Here I've teamed them with baby broad beans, cooked gently and tossed in olive oil, fresh lemon, spring onions, garlic and coriander.

tinted eggs with stewed baby broad beans

SERVES 4

4 eggs, scrubbed
Outer skins of 4 large onions
750 ml/1¼ pints/3 cups boiling
  water
225 g/8 oz shelled baby broad (fava)
  beans, thawed if frozen
150 ml/¼ pint/⅔ cup boiling
  vegetable or chicken stock
60 ml/4 tbsp olive oil
2 garlic cloves, crushed

Finely grated zest and juice of
  1 lemon
4 spring onions (scallions), chopped
Salt and freshly ground black pepper
A small handful of coriander
  (cilantro) leaves, torn into
  smallish pieces

TO SERVE:
Warm flat breads

1   Wrap the eggs in the onion skins, using elastic bands to secure them in place. Place in the crock pot and add the boiling water. Cover and cook on Low for at least 6 hours, preferably overnight. Remove from the pot and discard the water.

2   Put the beans in the pot with the boiling stock, the oil and garlic. Cover and cook on High for 1–2 hours until the beans are tender.

3   Add all the remaining ingredients except the coriander and eggs and mix well, seasoning to taste.

4   Discard the onion skins from the eggs and shell them. Spoon the warm beans and their juices into warm open soup plates. Halve the eggs and place on top. Sprinkle with the coriander and serve. To eat, mash the egg into the beans and scoop on to warm flat breads.

Black pudding is very popular, particularly in Spain and France. Here chick peas are cooked, then stewed gently with pieces of pudding, garlic and lots of fresh rosemary and parsley, then drizzled with extra virgin olive oil and fresh lemon juice. You can use a drained can of chick peas, if you prefer, in which case proceed from Step 3.

chick peas with black pudding, garlic and rosemary

SERVES 4

100 g/4 oz/⅔ cup dried chick peas (garbanzos), soaked in cold water for several hours or overnight
450 ml/¾ pint/2 cups boiling water
50 g/2 oz/⅓ cup raisins
30 ml/2 tbsp red wine
30 ml/2 tbsp extra virgin olive oil, plus extra for drizzling
1 onion, quartered and very thinly sliced

45 ml/3 tbsp pine nuts
1 garlic clove, finely chopped
100 g/4 oz black pudding, skinned and diced
1 large sprig of fresh rosemary, finely chopped
45 ml/3 tbsp chopped fresh parsley
Salt and freshly ground black pepper

TO SERVE:
Crusty bread

1 Drain the chick peas and place in a saucepan with the boiling water. Bring to the boil and boil rapidly for 10 minutes.

2 Tip into the crock pot, cover and cook on High for 3–4 hours until tender and most of the liquid has been absorbed.

3 Meanwhile, soak the raisins in the wine for at least 30 minutes until the fruit is plump and the wine has been absorbed.

4 Heat the oil in a small pan, add the onion and fry gently for 2 minutes to soften. Add the pine nuts and fry for 1 minute, stirring, until lightly golden.

5 Tip the mixture into the cooked chick peas in the pot and add the garlic, soaked raisins, black pudding, rosemary and half the parsley. Season well. Stir gently, re-cover and cook on High for 1 hour. Taste and re-season, if necessary.

6 Spoon the mixture on to warm plates, drizzle with olive oil and sprinkle with the remaining parsley. Serve with crusty bread.

MEAT-BASED
MAIN MEALS

Stews and casseroles are found in abundance around the Mediterranean. Magical mixtures of meat, vegetables, garlic, herbs and spices cooked gently to develop their wonderful flavours. Some are truly elegant affairs to impress family and friends, others rustic and hearty for everyday eating. You'll also find the most delicious lasagne recipe and an exciting change from moussaka – slices of aubergine wrapped around a rich lamb and Feta cheese filling, baked in the slow cooker then served with a chunky tomato and wine sauce. I bet you hadn't realised how versatile your crock pot could be!

Tagines come from Morocco. They are both the stew and the pots they are cooked in. Cooking is always long and slow, so tagines are ideal for making in your crock pot. They usually include sweet fruits along with the spices and savoury meat and vegetables – and always have a warm, rich flavour.

lamb tagine with almonds and apricots

SERVES 4

45 ml/3 tbsp olive oil
1 large onion, chopped
1 carrot, diced
1 celery stick, roughly chopped
2 garlic cloves, crushed
700 g/1½ lb lean diced lamb
2.5 cm/1 in piece of fresh root ginger, grated
5 ml/1 tsp ground cumin
5 ml/1 tsp ground coriander (cilantro)
1 cinnamon stick

100 g/4 oz/⅔ cup dried apricots, quartered
50 g/2 oz/½ cup whole blanched almonds
450 ml/¾ pint/2 cups lamb stock
Salt and freshly ground black pepper
2 courgettes (zucchini), diced
15 ml/1 tbsp tomato purée (paste)
10 ml/2 tsp clear honey

TO SERVE:
Couscous

1   Heat 15 ml/1 tbsp of the oil in a pan, add the onion, carrot, celery and garlic and fry for 2 minutes, stirring. Transfer to the crock pot with a draining spoon.

2   Heat the remaining oil, add the lamb in batches and fry to brown. Transfer to the crock pot.

3   Add the spices to the pan and fry, stirring, for 30 seconds. Add the apricots, almonds and stock and bring to the boil. Add to the crock pot, season well, then cover and cook on High for 3–4 hours until the lamb is tender.

4   Add the courgettes and stir in the tomato purée and honey. Cover and cook for a further 1 hour until the courgettes are just tender but still have some texture.

5   Season to taste, discard the cinnamon stick and serve with couscous.

This classic dish – called stifatho *or sometimes* stifadho *– is rich and warming. I like to serve it with a fluffy mash of mixed celeriac and potato, enriched with a good knob of butter and a spoonful of double cream, and a crisp green salad, but plain boiled potatoes and a green vegetable would also make good accompaniments, if you prefer.*

greek beef in red wine with baby onions and sweet spices

SERVES 4–6

45 ml/3 tbsp olive oil
1 kg/2¼ lb lean stewing steak, diced
16–24 pickling onions, peeled but
  left whole
1 large bay leaf
1 cinnamon stick
1 clove
1 thick lemon slice
2 garlic cloves, crushed

1 beefsteak tomato, skinned and
  chopped
15 ml/1 tbsp sun-dried tomato
  purée (paste)
250 ml/8 fl oz/1 cup red wine
30 ml/2 tbsp red wine vinegar
10 ml/2 tsp light brown sugar
Salt and freshly ground black pepper
30 ml/2 tbsp chopped fresh parsley,
  to garnish

1 Heat the oil in a large frying pan. Add the steak in batches and fry until browned all over. Transfer to the crock pot with a draining spoon.

2 Brown the onions quickly in the frying pan and transfer to the pot. Add the bay leaf, cinnamon stick and the clove, stuck in the lemon slice.

3 Put all the remaining ingredients in the frying pan and bring to the boil, stirring. Tip into the crock pot and stir well. Cover and cook on High for 4–5 hours until the steak is meltingly tender.

4 Taste and re-season, if necessary. Discard the bay leaf, cinnamon stick, clove and lemon and serve sprinkled with the parsley.

Pork cooked with coriander seeds and red wine is a Greek-Cypriot dish called afelia. *The same style of cooking is used for vegetables so here I've combined the two for a succulent, tender dish that needs only some buttered rice to finish it off – oh! and the crisp watercress and fennel salad I've included.*

pork with coriander seeds and baby courgettes and aubergines

SERVES 4

30 ml/2 tbsp olive oil
700 g/1½ lb lean diced pork
200 ml/7 fl oz/scant 1 cup red wine
5 ml/1 tsp tomato purée (paste)
5 ml/1 tsp clear honey
Salt and freshly ground black pepper
15 ml/1 tbsp coriander (cilantro) seeds, crushed
12 baby courgettes (zucchini), topped and tailed
12 baby aubergines (eggplants), trimmed

FOR THE SALAD:
1 bunch of watercress
1 head of fennel, quartered and thinly sliced
30 ml/2 tbsp olive oil
10 ml/2 tsp white balsamic condiment
2.5 ml/½ tsp Dijon mustard
2.5 ml/½ tsp dried oregano

1 Heat the oil in a frying pan, add the pork and brown on all sides. Tip into the crock pot.

2 Add the wine, tomato purée and honey to the pan and bring to the boil, scraping up any sediment. Add to the pork and season with salt and pepper.

3 Sprinkle the coriander seeds over and stir. Cover and cook on High for 2 hours.

4 Arrange the vegetables around the top, re-cover and cook on High for 2 hours until the meat is bathed in a rich sauce and very tender and the vegetables are cooked but still hold their shape. Taste and re-season if necessary.

5 Meanwhile, to make the salad, trim the watercress and put it in a bowl with the fennel. Whisk together the remaining ingredients with a little salt and pepper and pour over the salad. Toss and serve with the pork and vegetables.

This Italian speciality – bollito – is usually made in vast quantities with meats such as ox tongue and pig's cheek but here I've toned it down and used meats you are more likely to be familiar with. The result is still a fabulous hearty dish for carnivores! Use any leftover pesto to toss with pasta. How many it serves will depend very much on appetites!

peasant-style meat stew with mustard and pimiento pesto

SERVES 4–8

4 red onions, quartered
2 large carrots, thickly sliced
3 celery sticks, cut into chunks
1 small chicken, about 1.25 kg/
   2½ lb, cut into 8 pieces
450 g/1 lb piece of skirt beef or
   chuck steak, cut into 8 chunks
2 or 4 belly pork slices, halved
4–8 coarse meaty pork sausages
   (depending on number of
   servings)
1 bay leaf
Salt and freshly ground black pepper
600 ml/1 pint/2½ cups boiling water

FOR THE PESTO:
1 garlic clove, peeled and quartered
1 large or 2 small pimiento caps
   from a can or jar
2 sun-dried tomatoes, soaked in
   boiling water for 30 minutes
60 ml/4 tbsp pine nuts
30 ml/2 tbsp fresh thyme
15 ml/1 tbsp grated Parmesan
   cheese
Sprigs of fresh parsley, to garnish

TO SERVE:
Mustard (mild or hot according to
   taste) and plain boiled potatoes

1 Put all the vegetables in the crock pot and place all the meats on top. Add the bay leaf and season well. Add the boiling water, cover and cook on High for 5–6 hours.

2 Meanwhile, to make the pesto, blend all the ingredients to a coarse paste in a blender or food processor, stopping and scraping down the sides as necessary. Season to taste. Spoon into a small pot, and spoon some mustard into a second small pot.

3 When everything is cooked, carefully lift out the meats, then the vegetables with a draining spoon and arrange on a platter with the pots of pesto and mustard. Pour a little of the cooking broth into a warm jug.

4 Garnish the platter with sprigs of parsley and serve with plain boiled potatoes and the jug of broth handed separately.

This is a very simple dish that, although made with minced beef, benefits from long, slow cooking to become rich and very tender. Make sure you buy best-quality beef steak mince and don't overcook the spinach – it should be wilted, not a slimy mush, so it will need no longer than 30 minutes in the slow cooker.

turkish beef with spinach and spices

SERVES 4

30 ml/2 tbsp olive oil
A good knob of butter
1 bunch of spring onions (scallions), chopped
450 g/1 lb lean minced (ground) steak
1 large garlic clove, crushed
15 ml/1 tbsp paprika
5 ml/1 tsp ground allspice
5 ml/1 tsp ground cinnamon

2.5 ml/½ tsp crushed dried chillies (or more to taste)
300 ml/½ pint/1¼ cups thick plain yoghurt
300 g/11 oz fresh leaf spinach, well washed
Salt and freshly ground black pepper
225 g/8 oz/1⅓ cups bulghar (cracked wheat)
600 ml/1 pint/2½ cups boiling vegetable stock

1 Heat the oil and butter in a saucepan. Add the spring onions and mince and fry, stirring, until the meat grains are separate and no longer pink. Tip into the crock pot.

2 Stir the garlic, spices and half the yoghurt into the pot, cover and cook on Low for 3–4 hours until really tender.

3 Thirty minutes before you are ready to eat, stir in the spinach and season well. Re-cover and cook for 30 minutes until the spinach has wilted.

4 Meanwhile, put the bulghar in a pan with the boiling stock. Bring back to the boil, stir, cover and cook over a very gentle heat for 15 minutes until fluffy and all the liquid has been absorbed. Pile into warm shallow bowls, top with the meat and spinach and finish with a spoonful of the remaining yoghurt.

Kleftiko is one of my favourite lamb dishes. It is so easy to make and tastes just wonderful with a Greek-style salad that includes some Feta cheese, olives and juicy tomatoes. I've used lamb shanks but you could use a shoulder of lamb chopped in quarters or half a leg instead and cut it up after cooking.

greek lamb with garlic, oregano and potatoes

SERVES 4

4 lamb shanks
2 garlic cloves
8 potatoes, peeled and halved
5 ml/1 tsp dried oregano
Salt and freshly ground black pepper

200 ml/7 fl oz/scant 1 cup boiling
  lamb or chicken stock
A handful of black olives in olive oil
45 ml/3 tbsp chopped fresh parsley
Lemon wedges, to garnish

1 Make small slits with the point of a sharp knife in the lamb shanks. Cut the garlic into thin slivers and push a sliver into each slit. Place in the crock pot.

2 Arrange the potatoes all around. Sprinkle the lamb with the oregano and everything with some salt and pepper.

3 Pour in the stock and add the olives. Cover and cook on High for 5–6 hours until the lamb is meltingly tender and the potatoes are soft.

4 Carefully transfer the lamb and potatoes to warm plates. Spoon off any fat from the juices, then spoon them over the meat. Sprinkle with the parsley and garnish with lemon wedges before serving.

Daub de boeuf comes from Provence. It is hearty enough for a cold day but also elegant enough for a dinner party. I like the addition of butternut squash to bring a slight sweetness to the sauce, which is already enriched with anchovies. There shouldn't be too much sauce in the finished dish – the meat should just be nicely coated.

beef stew with tomatoes, orange and black olives

SERVES 4–6

50 g/2 oz unsmoked lardons (diced bacon)
1 kg/2¼ lb lean chuck steak, cut into 5 cm/2 in chunks
2 onions, chopped
2 large garlic cloves, crushed
2 carrots, diced
1 butternut squash, diced
2 beefsteak tomatoes, skinned and chopped
2 canned anchovy fillets, finely chopped
300 ml/½ pint/1¼ cups red wine

Finely grated zest and juice of 1 small orange
15 ml/1 tbsp tomato purée (paste)
15 ml/1 tbsp chopped fresh rosemary
1 bay leaf
Salt and freshly ground black pepper
16 black olives in oil, drained
Small sprigs of fresh rosemary, to garnish

TO SERVE:
Plain boiled rice or a mixture of camargue red and white long-grain rice

1 Place the lardons in a large frying pan and heat gently until the fat runs. Add the beef in batches and fry on all sides to brown. Transfer the beef and lardons to the crock pot with a draining spoon as you brown them.

2 Add the onions, garlic, carrots and squash to the pan and fry quickly for 2 minutes, stirring. Tip into the pan and add the tomatoes and anchovy fillets.

3 Pour the wine into the frying pan with the orange zest and juice and the tomato purée. Bring to the boil, stirring, and pour over the meat. Add the rosemary, bay leaf and some salt and pepper and stir well. Scatter the olives over.

4 Cover and cook on High for 4–5 hours until the meat is meltingly tender and the sauce is rich and thick. Taste and re-season.

5 Serve garnished with sprigs of rosemary on a bed of rice.

This is an exciting version of the classic Greek dish moussaka – but with a lovely modern twist. The aubergines are cut into long slices, wrapped round a fairly firm lamb and feta filling, delicately spiked with cinnamon and oregano, then bathed in a rich tomato sauce. Serve it with plain rice and a crisp salad.

aubergine wraps with lamb and feta

SERVES 4

4 aubergines (eggplants)
Olive oil
1 onion, very finely chopped
1 garlic clove, crushed
350 g/12 oz minced (ground) lamb
225 g/8 oz/2 cups crumbled Feta cheese
30 ml/2 tbsp sliced stoned (pitted) olives
2.5 ml/½ tsp ground cinnamon

5 ml/1 tsp dried oregano
30 ml/2 tbsp double (heavy) cream
Salt and freshly ground black pepper

FOR THE SAUCE:
450 g/1 lb ripe tomatoes, skinned and chopped
150 ml/¼ pint/⅔ cup dry white wine
15 ml/1 tbsp tomato purée (paste)
2.5 ml/½ tsp caster (superfine) sugar

1   Trim the stalks from the aubergines. Cut each aubergine lengthways into four slices.

2   Brush the aubergine slices all over with oil and either fry in a griddle pan for about 4 minutes on each side or in an electric griddle for about 4 minutes in all until they are striped brown on both sides and just tender. Leave to cool.

3   Heat 15 ml/1 tbsp of oil in a saucepan, add the onion and garlic and fry, stirring, for 3 minutes until softened and lightly golden. Stir in the lamb and cook until the grains are separate and no longer pink. Stir in the Feta, olives, cinnamon, oregano and cream and season to taste.

4   Lightly oil the crock pot. Spoon the mixture over the aubergine slices and roll up from the short end. With the end purple-sided slices, put the filling on the purple side. Carefully transfer to the crock pot, cover and cook on High for 1–2 hours.

5 Meanwhile, to make the sauce, put all the ingredients in a small saucepan, bring to the boil and boil rapidly, stirring occasionally, for 10 minutes or until the tomatoes are pulpy. Season to taste.

6 Transfer the aubergine rolls to plates and spoon a little tomato sauce over each one. Trickle with a little extra olive oil and serve warm.

You may not have thought of cooking a lasagne in your slow cooker but it works a treat as long as the sauces are quite thick, so it keeps its shape once cooked. The meat sauce makes a good Bolognese for spaghetti, too. Tip it into the slow cooker at step 2 (before simmering), then cook for 2–3 hours on High. You can use other red wine.

beef and chianti lasagne

SERVES 4

FOR THE MEAT SAUCE:
15 ml/1 tbsp olive oil, plus extra for greasing
1 large onion, finely chopped
350 g/12 oz lean minced (ground) steak
1 large garlic clove, crushed
1 carrot, finely diced
50 g/2 oz button mushrooms, sliced
60 ml/4 tbsp tomato purée (paste)
150 ml/¼ pint/⅔ cup Chianti
5 ml/1 tsp light brown sugar
2.5 ml/½ tsp dried oregano
1 bay leaf
1 lemon slice
Salt and freshly ground black pepper

FOR THE BÉCHAMEL SAUCE:
40 g/1½ oz/3 tbsp butter or margarine
40 g/1½ oz/⅓ cup plain (all-purpose) flour
450 ml/¾ pint/2 cups milk
5 ml/1 tsp dried mixed herbs

TO FINISH:
8 no-need-to-precook lasagne sheets
45 ml/3 tbsp grated Parmesan cheese

TO SERVE:
Garlic bread and a large mixed salad

1 To make the meat sauce, put the oil, onion, mince, garlic, carrot and mushrooms in a large saucepan and fry, stirring, until the beef is no longer pink and all the grains are separate.

2 Add the tomato purée, Chianti, sugar, oregano, bay leaf, lemon and some salt and pepper. Bring to the boil, stirring, reduce the heat and simmer for 5 minutes until the liquid has nearly evaporated and the sauce is thick. Taste and re-season, if necessary. Discard the bay leaf and lemon slice.

3 To make the béchamel sauce, melt the butter or margarine in a saucepan. Stir in the flour and cook, stirring, for 1 minute. Remove from the heat and gradually whisk in the milk until smooth. Add the herbs. Return to the heat, bring to the boil and cook for 2 minutes, stirring, until thick and smooth. Season to taste.

4 Oil the inside of the crock pot. Spread a little of the béchamel sauce in the base of the crock pot and top with two lasagne sheets. Add a third of the meat mixture, spreading it just over the sheets, then top with two more sheets. Repeat the layering until all the meat and lasagne is used, then spread the béchamel sauce over the top layer. Dust with the Parmesan, cover and cook on High for 1–2 hours.

5 Serve straight from the pot with garlic bread and a large mixed salad.

Tender slices of veal rolled around sweet-cured ham and a fresh sage and Gruyère cheese stuffing served on a bed of richly flavoured noodles. Use pork or turkey instead of veal, if you prefer, and serve the rest of the stock as soup, sprinkled with a little grated Parmesan. I use a food processor to chop the vegetables.

braised veal birds with cheese and ham on tomato noodles

SERVES 4

FOR THE VEAL BIRDS:
4 veal escalopes
4 thin slices of sweet-cured ham
50 g/2 oz/½ cup grated Gruyère (Swiss) cheese
50 g/2 oz/1 cup fresh breadcrumbs
15 ml/1 tbsp chopped fresh sage
Salt and freshly ground black pepper
1 egg, beaten

FOR THE BRAISE:
15 g/½ oz/1 tbsp butter
15 ml/1 tbsp olive oil
1 onion, very finely chopped
1 carrot, very finely chopped
1 turnip, very finely chopped

1 celery stick, very finely chopped
750 ml/1¼ pints/3 cups boiling chicken or vegetable stock
1 bouquet garni sachet

FOR THE TOMATO NOODLES:
350 g/12 oz tagliatelle
30 ml/2 tbsp olive oil
2 beefsteak tomatoes, skinned and finely chopped
1 garlic clove, crushed
30 ml/2 tbsp sun-dried tomato purée (paste)
15 ml/1 tbsp chopped fresh parsley, plus extra for garnishing

1 To make the veal birds, put the veal escalopes one at a time in a plastic bag and beat with a rolling pin or meat mallet to flatten. Lay a slice of ham on each.

2 Mix the cheese with the breadcrumbs, sage and some salt and pepper. Mix with the beaten egg to bind. Spread over the ham, then roll up each veal bird and secure with cocktail sticks (toothpicks).

3 To make the braise, melt the butter and oil in a large frying pan. Add the veal and brown quickly all over. Remove from the pan with a draining spoon and set aside.

4 Add the prepared vegetables to the pan and fry, stirring, for 2 minutes. Transfer to the crock pot.

5 Arrange the veal on top of the vegetables and add the stock and bouquet garni. Cover and cook on High for 2–3 hours.

6 To make the noodles, about 30 minutes before you are ready to serve, cook the tagliatelle according to the packet directions. Drain and return to the pan.

7 Heat the oil in a small saucepan, add the chopped tomatoes and garlic and cook for about 5 minutes, stirring, until the tomatoes are soft and pulpy. Stir in the tomato purée and parsley, tip into the noodles and toss well. Pile on to plates.

8 Carefully lift the veal out of the pot. Remove the cocktail sticks and slice the birds thickly. Arrange the slices at the side of the noodles and spoon a little of the vegetable braise over. Sprinkle with a little chopped parsley and serve hot.

*This is always served with little triangles of fried bread as a garnish –
don't ask me why, it just is! Kidneys are an often-forgotten meat that are
not only highly nutritious but very inexpensive too. The sweetness of
the port and the saltiness of the bacon and sausages complement the
kidneys perfectly.*

kidneys with port, baby sausages and bacon

SERVES 4

15 ml/1 tbsp olive oil
12 button (pearl) onions, peeled but
  left whole
12 lamb's kidneys, quartered and
  cored
16 cocktail sausages
30 ml/2 tbsp plain (all-purpose) flour
90 ml/6 tbsp ruby port
150 ml/¼ pint/⅔ cup beef stock
15 ml/1 tbsp chopped fresh thyme
Salt and freshly ground black pepper
60 ml/4 tbsp crème fraîche

FOR THE GARNISH:
4 rashers (slices) of streaky bacon,
  rinded
30 ml/2 tbsp olive oil
25 g/1 oz/2 tbsp butter
1 slice of white bread, crusts
  removed and cut into 4 triangles
15 ml/1 tbsp chopped fresh parsley

TO SERVE:
Plain boiled rice and French (green)
beans

1   Heat the oil in a frying pan, add the onions and brown them
    quickly. Remove with a draining spoon and place in the crock pot.

2   Add the kidneys to the pan and brown quickly. Transfer to the
    crock pot with the draining spoon.

3   Add the sausages to the pan and brown quickly. Transfer to the
    crock pot with the draining spoon.

4   Spoon off all but 15 ml/1 tbsp of the fat from the pan. Stir in the
    flour, port and stock and bring to the boil, stirring. Pour into the
    crock pot and add the thyme and some salt and pepper. Cover and
    cook on High for 2–3 hours until the kidneys are tender and
    bathed in a rich sauce.

5   Meanwhile, make the garnish. Roll up the bacon, secure with
    cocktail sticks (toothpicks) if liked, then fry in a frying pan until
    golden and fairly crisp, turning as necessary. Drain on kitchen
    paper (paper towels) and keep warm.

6 Heat the oil and butter in the same pan, add the bread triangles and fry on both sides until golden. Remove from the pan and drain on kitchen paper. Dip the point of each triangle in the parsley.

7 Stir the crème fraîche into the crock pot, taste and re-season, if necessary. Serve on a bed of rice with French beans and garnish each plate with a fried bread triangle and a twist of bacon roll.

This Italian dish comes from the rugged region of Calabria and is called braciole di maiale in salsa. *It was created as an easy way to cook meat with minimum fuss and maximum flavour! You could use braising steak instead of the chops for* braciole di manzo. *Potato gnocchi is the perfect accompaniment.*

braised pork chops in tomato, chilli and caper sauce

SERVES 4

45 ml/3 tbsp plain (all-purpose) flour
Salt and freshly ground black pepper
4 large pork loin chops
60 ml/4 tbsp olive oil
1 garlic clove, crushed
15 ml/1 tbsp chopped pickled
   capers
1 red chilli, seeded and chopped
4 tomatoes, skinned and chopped

150 ml/¼ pint/⅔ cup red wine
75 ml/5 tbsp red wine vinegar
75 ml/5 tbsp water
5 ml/1 tsp caster (superfine) sugar
1 bay leaf
1 sprig of fresh rosemary

TO SERVE:
Potato gnocchi

1   Mix the flour with a little salt and pepper and use to coat the chops.

2   Heat the oil in a frying pan, add the pork and fry quickly on both sides to brown. Transfer to the crock pot with a draining spoon and scatter the garlic, capers and chilli over.

3   Tip the tomatoes, wine, vinegar and water into the pan. Stir in the sugar and a little more salt and pepper. Bring to the boil and pour over the chops.

4   Add the bay leaf and rosemary, cover and cook on High for 3–4 hours until the pork is really tender. Discard the bay leaf and rosemary and taste and re-season, if necessary. Serve with potato gnocchi.

POULTRY-BASED
MAIN MEALS

Although chicken and other poultry don't take that long to cook conventionally, they can sometimes be dry from being overdone. But cooking them in your slow cooker will render them moist, tender and meltingly delicious every time. The birds won't dry out if you leave them longer in the cooker but the meat will, literally, fall off the bones! Always cook on Low if you aren't quite sure when you'll be ready to eat. Here you'll find slow-cooked versions of some wonderful traditional specialities such as *piri piri chicken* and *coq au vin* but there are also some exciting new versions of Mediterranean dishes, like my Stewed Duck with Pears and Serrano Ham or Guinea Fowl with Peppers and Sun-dried Tomatoes. All are perfect for your slow cooker; all taste out of this world.

This dish is said to have been made for Napoleon when he beat the Austrians at the Battle of Marengo in 1800. It was part of the celebratory feast prepared by his chef who had to improvise with what he had to hand – a hen, some garlic, tomatoes, eggs and a few crayfish! I've made a few changes and additions, but the essence of the dish is still there.

chicken marengo with langoustines and fried eggs

SERVES 4

60 ml/4 tbsp olive oil
15 g/½ oz/1 tbsp butter
4 chicken portions
100 g/4 oz whole baby button
  mushrooms
1 large onion, finely chopped
2 large garlic cloves, crushed
15 ml/1 tbsp cornflour (cornstarch)
15 ml/1 tbsp water
4 large, ripe tomatoes, skinned and
  chopped

150 ml/¼ pint/⅔ cup dry white wine
150 ml/¼ pint/⅔ cup chicken stock
30 ml/2 tbsp tomato purée (paste)
1 bay leaf
Salt and freshly ground black pepper
4 slices of French bread
4 cooked langoustines
4 eggs
30 ml/2 tbsp chopped fresh parsley

1 Heat 15 ml/1 tbsp of the oil and the butter in a frying pan, add the chicken portions and brown on all sides. Transfer to the crock pot with a draining spoon. Add the mushrooms to the pot.

2 Add the onion and garlic to the frying pan and fry for 2 minutes, stirring. Transfer to the crock pot with a draining spoon. Mix the cornflour with the water and chopped tomatoes and add to the pot.

3 Blend the wine, stock and tomato purée in the frying pan. Bring to the boil, stirring, then pour over the chicken. Tuck in the bay leaf and season well. Cover and cook on High for 3–4 hours until the chicken is really tender.

4 Just before you are ready to serve, fry the French bread in half the remaining oil until golden on both sides. Wipe out the pan with kitchen paper (paper towels). Toss the langoustines in the pan until hot, then transfer to a plate and set aside to keep warm.

5 Heat the remaining oil in the pan, add the eggs and fry to your liking.

6 Transfer the chicken to warm plates with a draining spoon. Stir the juices, taste and re-season, if necessary. Spoon over the chicken. Put a slice of fried French bread on each plate and top with an egg. Lay a langoustine alongside and garnish the chicken with the chopped parsley.

This is a selection of the best Mediterranean fare, braised together to create a stew worthy of France, Italy or Spain. Choose a well-flavoured white wine, such as a Chardonnay, for this recipe – and enjoy the rest of it chilled to accompany the meal. A delicious dish that couldn't be simpler to prepare!

chicken stew with artichokes, leeks and potatoes

SERVES 4

15 ml/1 tbsp olive oil
4 chicken portions
2 leeks, cut into chunks
4 potatoes, cut into walnut-sized
  pieces
120 ml/4 fl oz/½ cup dry white wine
120 ml/4 fl oz/½ cup chicken stock

Salt and freshly ground black pepper
280 g/10 oz jar of chargrilled
  artichoke hearts in oil, drained
2 garlic cloves, finely chopped
30 ml/2 tbsp chopped fresh parsley

TO SERVE:
A crisp green salad

1 Heat the oil in a frying pan, add the chicken portions and brown quickly on all sides. Transfer to the crock pot with a draining spoon.

2 Add the leeks and potatoes to the pan and toss gently over a fairly high heat until lightly golden. Transfer to the pot.

3 Add the wine and stock to the pan and bring to the boil. Pour into the pot and season well. Cover and cook on High for 3–4 hours until everything is tender.

4 Taste the stew 5 minutes before eating. Re-season, if necessary, add the artichokes and sprinkle the garlic and parsley over. Re-cover and cook for the final 5 minutes. Serve straight from the pot with a crisp green salad.

This is a classic – coq au vin. It is sometimes made with red wine but I prefer the subtle flavour of a white burgundy. The chicken is gently cooked in the wine with lardons, shallots and robust chestnut mushrooms. It is traditionally served with crusty French bread to mop up the juices and a crisp green salad.

chicken in white burgundy with shallots and chestnut mushrooms

SERVES 4

15 g/½ oz/1 tbsp butter
15 ml/1 tbsp olive oil
4 chicken portions
50 g/2 oz lardons (diced bacon)
12 shallots, peeled but left whole
100 g/4 oz chestnut mushrooms, quartered if large
60 ml/4 tbsp plain flour
5 ml/1 tsp dark brown sugar

250 ml/8 fl oz/1 cup white burgundy, such as Chardonnay or Macon
200 ml/7 fl oz/scant 1 cup chicken stock
Salt and freshly ground black pepper
1 bouquet garni sachet
30 ml/2 tbsp chopped fresh parsley, to garnish

1 Heat the butter and oil in a large frying pan, add the chicken portions and brown on all sides. Transfer to the crock pot with a draining spoon.

2 Add the lardons, shallots and mushrooms to the pan and fry, stirring, until lightly browned. Transfer to the pot with the draining spoon.

3 Stir the flour and sugar into the pan juices and cook, stirring, for 2 minutes until nicely browned. Remove from the heat and blend in the wine and stock. Return to the heat and bring to the boil, stirring. Season to taste and pour over the chicken.

4 Tuck in the bouquet garni, cover and cook on High for 3–4 hours.

5 Discard the bouquet garni. Taste and re-season, if necessary. Garnish with the parsley before serving.

A fricassee just means the dish is cooked in white sauce. But if that sounds bland and boring this dish is far from that. The pieces of chicken breast are slowly cooked in stock with a colourful selection of vegetables. Then sherry and double cream are added and the fricassee is served on a bed of buttered rice. It is delicate but full of flavour.

chicken fricassee with spring vegetables

SERVES 4

100 g/4 oz baby corn cobs
1 bunch of spring onions (scallions), cut into short lengths
100 g/4 oz baby carrots, trimmed and halved lengthways if thick
100 g/4 oz whole button mushrooms
4 small turnips, quartered
450 ml/¾ pint/2 cups boiling chicken stock
45 ml/3 tbsp dry sherry

Salt and freshly ground black pepper
1 bouquet garni sachet
45 ml/3 tbsp cornflour (cornstarch)
45 ml/3 tbsp water
4 skinless chicken breasts, cut into chunks
100 g/4 oz mangetout (snow peas)
90 ml/6 tbsp double (heavy) cream
30 ml/2 tbsp chopped fresh parsley

TO SERVE:
Buttered rice

1 Put the corn, spring onions, carrots, mushrooms and turnips in the crock pot.

2 Add the stock, sherry and some seasoning and tuck in the bouquet garni. Cover and cook on High for 1–2 hours.

3 Blend the cornflour with the water and stir into the pot. Add the chicken and mangetout and cook for a further 1 hour.

4 Stir in the cream and discard the bouquet garni. Taste and re-season, if necessary.

5 Serve the fricassee on a bed of buttered rice, garnished with the chopped parsley.

This lovely moist rice dish from Spain has chunky pieces of (
chorizo sausage, garlic and red peppers. Pimentón – smoked
really enhances the flavour and is so characteristic of the cou
pieces of chicken with the bone in as it really adds to the flav
keeps the meat juicy and tender. Serve as soon as it's cooked.

chicken paella with chorizo and peppers

SERVES 4–6

2 or 3 chicken portions or 4–6 chicken thighs
15 ml/1 tbsp olive oil
2 red (bell) peppers, diced
100 g/4 oz chorizo sausage, skinned and diced
100 g/4 oz button mushrooms, sliced
1 onion, chopped
2 garlic cloves, crushed
350 g/12 oz/1½ cups paella or long-grain rice

1 litre/1¾ pints/4¼ cups chicken stock
2.5 ml/½ tsp pimentón
2.5 ml/½ tsp ground turmeric
5 ml/1 tsp dried oregano
Salt and freshly ground black pepper
30 ml/2 tbsp chopped fresh parsley and lemon wedges, to garnish

TO SERVE:
Garlic bread and a crisp green salad

1 Chop chicken portions into four pieces or thighs into two pieces, using a meat cleaver or a heavy knife and a weight.

2 Heat the oil in a large frying pan, add the chicken and brown all over. Transfer to the crock pot with a draining spoon and add the peppers, chorizo and mushrooms.

3 Add the onion and garlic to the pan and fry, stirring, for 2 minutes until they are softened but not browned.

4 Add the rice to the pan and stir until glistening in oil. Add the stock, pimentón, turmeric, oregano and some salt and pepper. Bring to the boil, stirring, and tip into the crock pot. Cover and cook on Low for 2 hours until the rice has absorbed the liquid and the chicken is tender.

5 Fluff up the rice with a fork, taste and re-season, if necessary. Spoon into warm shallow bowls, garnish with chopped parsley and lemon wedges and serve with garlic bread and a crisp green salad.

This classic Turkish dish dates back to the time of the Ottoman Empire. It was originally made with fresh walnuts, so do use them if you have a walnut tree in your garden (you will need to pick them when they are still young and quite 'milky') but I love this version made with pale green pistachios.

poached chicken
with pistachio sauce

SERVES 4

1 small oven-ready chicken, about
    1.25 kg/2½ lb
1 onion, quartered
1 carrot, cut into chunks
1 celery stick, cut into chunks
6 peppercorns
1 bay leaf
1 star anise
Salt and freshly ground black pepper
Boiling water
50 g/2 oz/½ cup shelled pistachio
    nuts

1 white pitta bread, cut into pieces
1 small garlic clove, crushed
30 ml/2 tbsp single (light) cream
450 g/1 lb fresh spinach leaves
15 ml/1 tbsp olive oil
15 ml/1 tbsp sweet paprika
1.5 ml/¼ tsp chilli powder

TO SERVE:
Plain boiled potatoes

1 Pull off and discard any excess fat from around the inside of the body cavity of the chicken. Place the bird in the crock pot. Add the prepared vegetables, the peppercorns, bay leaf, star anise, some salt and pepper and 450 ml/¾ pint/2 cups of boiling water. Cover and cook on High for 3–4 hours.

2 Meanwhile, to make the sauce, soak the pistachios in 45 ml/3 tbsp of boiling water for at least 30 minutes to soften. Transfer to a food processor and add the bread and garlic. Run the machine, stopping and scraping down the sides as necessary, until the mixture is finely processed. Transfer to a large bowl.

3 Carefully lift the chicken out of the pot and, when cool enough to handle, remove all the meat from the bones and discard the skin. Cut the meat into neat pieces and keep warm. Strain the stock and reserve.

4 Gradually blend the strained stock with the pistachio mixture to form a thick sauce. Blend in the cream and season to taste. Stir the chicken into the sauce, then return everything to the crock pot to keep warm on Low.

5 Quickly pour boiling water over the spinach in a colander and toss to wilt it. Drain thoroughly. Pile the spinach on to warm plates and spoon the chicken and sauce over. Blend the oil with the paprika and chilli powder and trickle over. Serve this dish warm (not boiling hot) with plain boiled potatoes.

Poussins, also known as spring chickens, are now farmed all year round. They make a delicious dinner party treat. To cook four poussins, you need a large slow cooker. You can halve the recipe and cook two birds on top of each other in a smaller pot. This recipe is very simple but the flavours are truly Mediterranean – lemon, basil, garlic and white wine.

spatchcocked poussins with lemon and pesto

SERVES 4

4 oven-ready poussins (Cornish
   hens)
60 ml/4 tbsp basil pesto from a jar
30 ml/2 tbsp olive oil
1 lemon, thinly sliced
1 garlic clove, cut into thin slivers
15 ml/1 tbsp cornflour (cornstarch)

90 ml/6 tbsp dry white wine
90 ml/6 tbsp chicken stock
Salt and freshly ground black pepper
Lemon twists and sprigs of fresh
   basil, to garnish

TO SERVE:
Buttered tagliatelle

1 To spatchcock the poussins, cut them each side of the backbone. Remove the backbone and open the birds out flat. Carefully loosen the skin and smear the pesto between the flesh and the skin.

2 Heat the oil in a frying pan, add the poussins and fry quickly to brown. Transfer to the crock pot. Tuck the lemon slices and garlic slivers around. Blend the cornflour with 15 ml/1 tbsp of the wine and add to the crock pot.

3 Add the remaining wine and the stock to the frying pan. Bring to the boil, stirring, and pour over the poussins. Season well. Cover and cook on High for 2–3 hours until tender.

4 Remove the chicken from the pot with a draining spoon. Stir, taste and re-season the sauce, if necessary.

5 Serve the chicken on a bed of buttered tagliatelle, with the sauce spooned over, garnished with lemon twists and sprigs of basil.

This dish is very French. The simple sweet flavours of peas, fresh herbs and lettuce offset the richness of the duck to perfection. It needs very little accompaniment except, perhaps, some plain boiled potatoes. When partridges are in season, try cooking them in the same way; you would need one bird per person.

braised duck with lettuce and petit pois

SERVES 4

4 duck portions
12 button (pearl) onions, peeled but left whole
45 ml/3 tbsp cornflour (cornstarch)
45 ml/3 tbsp water
300 ml/½ pint/1¼ cups boiling chicken stock
Salt and freshly ground black pepper

225 g/8 oz/2 cups frozen petit pois, thawed
30 ml/2 tbsp chopped fresh mint
15 ml/1 tbsp chopped fresh oregano
15 ml/1 tbsp chopped fresh parsley
1 round lettuce, shredded
Small sprigs of fresh mint, to garnish

1 Heat a large heavy-based frying pan. Turn down the heat to moderate, add the duck, skin-sides down, and heat gently until the fat runs. Turn up the heat and brown the duck all over. Transfer to the crock pot with a draining spoon.

2 Add the onions to the pan and brown quickly. Add to the duck, using the draining spoon.

3 Blend the cornflour with the water, then stir in the boiling stock. Pour over the duck. Season with salt and pepper, cover and cook on High for 2–3 hours.

4 Add the petit pois, herbs and lettuce. Cover and cook for a further 1 hour.

5 Transfer the duck to warm plates. Spoon off the excess fat from the peas and juices. Taste and re-season, if necessary. Spoon over the duck and garnish with small sprigs of mint.

Confit de canard is actually a speciality of Gascony, which is not on the Med – but it isn't that far away and it's too good a recipe to miss here as the slow cooker makes it perfectly. I've used oils rather than the traditional duck fat. It is an ancient way of preserving the meat and it will keep for ages in the fridge as long as it is totally submerged in the oil.

gascon confit
of duck

SERVES 4

4 duck leg portions
25 g/1 oz/¼ cup salt
2 large garlic cloves, crushed
8 black peppercorns, lightly crushed
A good pinch of ground cloves
5 ml/1 tsp dried thyme
2 bay leaves, torn into pieces
500 ml/17 fl oz/2¼ cups olive oil

500 ml/17 fl oz/2¼ cups sunflower oil

TO SERVE:
A chicory (Belgian endive), watercress and orange salad and crusty French bread

1   Put the duck portions in a large shallow plastic container and rub the salt all over. Add the garlic, spices and herbs and mix well so they are evenly distributed. Cover with a lid and chill for 24 hours.

2   Wash the duck thoroughly under cold water and pat dry on kitchen paper (paper towels). This is very important or the finished dish will be too salty. Arrange the duck in the crock pot.

3   Heat the oils in a saucepan until hot but not boiling. Pour over the duck. Cover and cook on Low for 4–5 hours until the duck is meltingly tender.

4   Remove the crock pot from its base and leave until fairly cool. Carefully transfer the duck to a suitable container that can be kept in the fridge and pour all the oil over to cover it completely. When completely cold, store in the fridge.

5   To serve, carefully take the duck out of the oil. Heat a large heavy-based frying pan and fry the duck until crisp and golden on the outside and piping hot. Serve with a chicory, watercress and orange salad and some crusty French bread.

This is a lovely version of canard à l'orange, *where the duck is flavoured with orange marmalade as well as fresh orange juice and zest. The rosemary gives added fragrance and, when served with plain new potatoes and petit pois, makes a perfect, simple, special occasion meal.*

duck with wine, rosemary and orange sauce

SERVES 4

1.75 kg/4 lb oven-ready duck,
   quartered, or 4 duck portions
5 ml/1 tsp chopped fresh rosemary
200 ml/7 fl oz/scant 1 cup chicken
   stock
200 ml/7 fl oz/scant 1 cup dry white
   wine
30 ml/2 tbsp orange jelly marmalade

Finely grated zest and juice of
   1 large orange
Salt and freshly ground black pepper
45 ml/3 tbsp cornflour (cornstarch)
45 ml/3 tbsp water
4 small sprigs of fresh rosemary and
   4 orange slices, to garnish

1 Heat a large heavy-based frying pan. Turn down the heat to moderate, add the duck, skin-sides down, and heat gently until the fat runs. Turn up the heat and brown the duck all over. Transfer to the crock pot with a draining spoon.

2 Add the rosemary, stock, wine, marmalade, orange zest and juice and some salt and pepper to the pan. Bring to the boil, stirring, until the marmalade melts. Blend the cornflour with the water and stir in. Cook until thickened, then pour over the duck. Cover and cook on High for 3–4 hours until tender.

3 Spoon off any fat from the cooking juices in the crock pot. Taste and re-season, if necessary. Transfer the duck to warm plates and spoon the sauce around. Garnish each piece of duck with a small sprig of rosemary and an orange slice and serve hot.

This comes from Catalonia in Spain and has a wonderful mixture of flavours and textures. In Spain they often cook the dish one day, then cool and chill it so all the fat can be scraped off the following day before reheating. I find spooning it off then blotting the surface with kitchen paper works equally well and also means you can enjoy it sooner!

stewed duck with pears and serrano ham

SERVES 4

1.75 kg/4 lb oven-ready duck, quartered, or 4 duck portions
1 onion, halved and thinly sliced
1 garlic clove, crushed
2 thin slices of Serrano ham, cut into thin strips
50 g/2 oz/½ cup blanched almonds
50 g/2 oz/⅓ cup sultanas (golden raisins)
A pinch of ground cloves
15 ml/1 tbsp chopped fresh sage

150 ml/¼ pint/⅔ cup chicken stock
300 ml/½ pint/1¼ cups apple juice
15 ml/1 tbsp Spanish brandy
Salt and freshly ground black pepper
15 ml/1 tbsp sherry vinegar
4 eating (dessert) pears, peeled, cored and quartered
A few fresh sage leaves, to garnish

TO SERVE:
Plain boiled rice

1   Heat a large heavy-based frying pan. Turn down the heat to moderate, add the duck, skin-sides down, and heat gently until the fat runs. Turn up the heat and brown the duck all over. Transfer to the crock pot with a draining spoon.

2   Add the onion and garlic to the pan and fry, stirring, for 2 minutes until the onion is softened and lightly browned. Transfer to the pot with a draining spoon and add the ham, almonds, sultanas, cloves and sage.

3   Wipe out the frying pan with kitchen paper (paper towels). Add the stock, apple juice and brandy, bring to the boil and pour into the pot. Season well. Cover and cook on High for 3–4 hours until really tender.

4 Carefully lift the duck out of the pot. Spoon off as much fat as possible from the cooking liquid, then lay a sheet of kitchen paper on the surface to soak up the remaining fat (you may need to repeat this). Stir the sherry vinegar into the juices, taste and re-season, if necessary. Return the duck to the pot with the pears and cook for a further 30 minutes.

5 Serve on a bed of rice, garnished with a few sage leaves.

Guinea fowl were introduced to the Mediterranean in ancient times but were first discovered in the Sahara in Africa. They are now farmed all over Europe. Here they are slow cooked on a bed of sweet peppers, with garlic and sun-dried tomatoes. They are served with couscous to create a delicious Middle Eastern-style dish.

guinea fowl with peppers and sun-dried tomatoes

SERVES 4

5 ml/1 tsp ground cumin
2.5 ml/½ tsp ground cinnamon
Salt and freshly ground black pepper
1 oven-ready guinea fowl, quartered
60 ml/4 tbsp olive oil
1 onion, halved and sliced
2 red (bell) peppers, cut into 8 strips
2 green peppers, cut into 8 strips
2 garlic cloves, crushed

4 sun-dried tomatoes in olive oil, drained and chopped
15 ml/1 tbsp sun-dried tomato oil
15 ml/1 tbsp chopped fresh coriander (cilantro)
A few coriander leaves, to garnish

TO SERVE:
Couscous

1 Mix the cumin and cinnamon with 2.5 ml/½ tsp of salt. Rub all over the guinea fowl pieces.

2 Heat the oil in a frying pan, add the onion and fry for 2 minutes, stirring. Transfer to the crock pot with a draining spoon. Add the peppers, garlic, sun-dried tomatoes and the sun-dried tomato oil. Toss well and spread out. Season with a little salt and lots of pepper.

3 Place the guinea fowl in the frying pan and brown all over. Transfer to the pot and pour over all the juices from the pan. Cover and cook on High for 3–4 hours until everything is meltingly tender.

4 Stir in the coriander. Taste and re-season, if necessary. Transfer to warm plates on a bed of couscous and garnish with coriander leaves.

Frango piri piri originated in Mongolia but is now a popular Portuguese dish. It's often marinated then barbecued, but I've slow cooked it then popped it under the grill to brown and crisp the skin. Because it is slow cooked, you don't need to marinate it first as the flavours have plenty of time to penetrate. Vary the amount of chilli you use to taste.

portuguese-style chicken
with chillies

SERVES 4

1 garlic clove, crushed
5 ml/1 tsp dried oregano
2.5–10 ml/½–2 tsp crushed dried
   chillies
5 ml/1 tsp paprika
2.5 ml/½ tsp salt
A good grinding of black pepper
90 ml/6 tbsp olive oil

60 ml/4 tbsp red wine vinegar
5 ml/1 tsp caster (superfine) sugar
4 chicken portions
30 ml/2 tbsp chopped fresh parsley

TO SERVE:
Sautéed potatoes and a large mixed
salad

1   Put the garlic, oregano, chillies, paprika, salt, pepper, oil, vinegar and sugar in a saucepan and bring to the boil. Reduce the heat and simmer for 2 minutes.

2   Make several slashes in each piece of the chicken, place in the crock pot and pour the chilli mixture over. Cover and cook on High for 2 hours.

3   Preheat the grill (broiler). Carefully lift out the chicken and transfer it, skin-sides down, to the grill. Grill (broil) for 5 minutes. Turn the chicken over and grill for a further 5–10 minutes until crisp and golden, brushing with the cooking juices from the crock pot during grilling.

4   Serve sprinkled with the parsley, with sautéed potatoes and a large mixed salad.

FISH-BASED
MAIN MEALS

The Mediterranean is famous for its fish. You'll find lots of it grilled or barbecued with garlic and herbs and served simply with lots of fresh lemons to squeeze over. However, there are numerous fish dishes that are fabulous slow cooked at home. Here are my adaptations of some of the most popular ones. You'll find everything from Salmon Poached in Champagne to Stewed Squid Rings with Peppers and Chilli Flakes. I guarantee that every one of them will widen your horizons and develop your taste buds. We should all eat more fish for a balanced diet and here is a way of doing it effortlessly and deliciously!

Halibut is one of my favourite fish. Its meaty, firm and sweet flesh makes it the perfect fish for the slow cooker as it is thick enough to cook gently without drying out or falling apart. Wrapping the fillets in Parma ham imparts a glorious Italian flavour and the puy lentils are the perfect base to cook it on.

halibut wrapped in parma ham on a puy lentil braise

SERVES 4

60 ml/4 tbsp olive oil
1 red onion, halved and thinly sliced
1 aubergine (eggplant), diced
1 garlic clove, crushed
1 large carrot, diced
1 head of fennel, diced
350 g/12 oz/2 cups puy lentils
300 ml/½ pint/1¼ cups red wine
900 ml/1½ pints/3¾ cups fish or
   chicken stock

30 ml/2 tbsp tomato purée (paste)
5 ml/1 tsp caster (superfine) sugar
Salt and freshly ground black pepper
8 fresh sage leaves, plus extra small
   ones for garnishing
4 pieces of halibut fillet, about
   150 g/5 oz each
4 thin slices of Parma ham

TO SERVE:
Crusty bread and a crisp green salad

1　Heat the oil in a frying pan, add the onion, aubergine, garlic, carrot and fennel and fry, stirring, for 2 minutes. Tip into the crock pot and add the lentils.

2　Pour the wine and stock into the pan and bring to the boil. Stir in the tomato purée and sugar, then pour over the lentils. Season well. Cover and cook on High for 3 hours until the lentils are almost tender.

3　Meanwhile, put two sage leaves on each piece of fish. Season well with pepper. Wrap each piece in a slice of Parma ham.

4　When the lentils are cooked, turn down the slow cooker to Low. Place the fish on top of the lentils with the end flap of ham underneath. Re-cover and cook for a further 1 hour until the fish is tender.

5　Carefully lift the fish off the lentils and cut each into thick slices. Spoon the lentils on to warm plates, lay the fish slices on top and garnish with a few small sage leaves. Serve with crusty bread and a crisp green salad.

I first had this in Cyprus in the early 1980s. It is a popular way of cooking all types of whole fish but particularly mullet and bream. It is a very simple dish that brings out the full flavour of the fish and makes a substantial main meal when served with some dishes of olives and gherkins and perhaps some radishes.

baked red mullet with tomatoes, celeriac and potatoes

SERVES 4

2 large potatoes, peeled and cut into thin fingers
1 small celeriac (celery root), peeled and cut into thin fingers
4 red mullet, cleaned and scaled
Salt and freshly ground black pepper
1 lemon, quartered
150 ml/¼ pint/⅔ cup olive oil
100 g/4 oz/2 cups fresh breadcrumbs

30 ml/2 tbsp chopped fresh parsley
2 garlic cloves, finely chopped
1 lemon, thinly sliced
900 g/2 lb ripe tomatoes, thickly sliced
Lemon wedges and sprigs of fresh parsley, to garnish

TO SERVE:
Crusty bread

1   Parboil the potatoes and celeriac in lightly salted water for 2–3 minutes or until almost tender. Drain well.

2   Rub the fish all over with salt and the lemon.

3   Heat the oil until hot but no boiling. Pour enough into the crock pot to cover the base. Sprinkle with the breadcrumbs, parsley and garlic and season lightly.

4   Lay the potato and celeriac pieces in the crock pot. Lay the fish over and top each with a lemon slice. Top everything with a layer of tomato slices and pour the rest of the oil over. Season well with pepper. Cover and cook on Low for 2 hours until the fish and vegetables are tender.

5   Leave to cool slightly, then serve warm, garnished with lemon wedges and sprigs of parsley, with crusty bread.

This French dish is one of my favourite ways of serving fish. The firm, meaty monkfish is cooked very gently with a medley of vegetables in a white wine sauce laced with Pernod and enriched with crème fraîche. You can vary the vegetables as you like and use different fish such as cod loin or even thick pieces of salmon.

poached monkfish with spring vegetables in a creamy pernod sauce

SERVES 4

25 g/1 oz/2 tbsp unsalted (sweet) butter
1 onion, finely chopped
1 garlic clove, crushed
50 g/2 oz smoked lardons (diced bacon)
1 large carrot, diced
1 turnip, diced
1 head of fennel, chopped
150 ml/¼ pint/⅔ cup dry white wine
150 ml/¼ pint/⅔ cup fish stock

30 ml/2 tbsp Pernod
Salt and freshly ground black pepper
100 g/4 oz/1 cup frozen petit pois, thawed
100 g/4 oz asparagus spears, cut into short lengths
700 g/1½ lb monkfish, cut into large chunks
90 ml/6 tbsp crème fraîche

TO SERVE:
French bread

1   Melt the butter in a large frying pan, add the onion, garlic, lardons and carrot and fry gently, stirring, for 2 minutes. Tip into the crock pot and add the turnip and fennel.

2   Add the wine, stock and Pernod to the pan, bring to the boil, then pour over the vegetables. Season well. Cover and cook on High for 2 hours. Turn the pot to Low.

3   Add the petit pois, asparagus and the fish. Re-cover and cook on Low for a further 1–2 hours until the fish and all the vegetables are tender.

4   Carefully lift the monkfish and vegetables out of the pot with a draining spoon and transfer to warm shallow bowls. Stir the crème fraîche into the cooking liquid. Taste and re-season, if necessary. Spoon over the fish and vegetables and serve straight away with French bread.

In the South of France, you'll find versions of this Provençal dish made with all manner of fresh seafood. You can substitute any other white meaty fish or even raw prawns for the cod. You could also make it with chicken breasts instead of fish, though you would need to cook it on High for 3 hours.

provençal cod with tomatoes and olives

SERVES 4

30 ml/2 tbsp olive oil
1 large onion, chopped
2 celery sticks, chopped
2 garlic cloves, crushed
4 beefsteak tomatoes, skinned and
    chopped
150 ml/¼ pint/⅔ cup dry white wine
30 ml/2 tbsp sun-dried tomato
    purée (paste)
2.5 ml/½ tsp dried herbes de
    Provence

700 g/1½ lb cod fillet, skinned and
    cut into chunks
50 g/2 oz black olives, stoned
    (pitted), if preferred
Salt and freshly ground black pepper
30 ml/2 tbsp chopped fresh parsley

TO SERVE:
Plain boiled rice

1   Heat the oil in a frying pan, add the onion, celery and garlic and fry gently, stirring, for 5 minutes until softened but not browned. Add the tomatoes, wine, tomato purée and herbs and bring to the boil.

2   Put the cod in the crock pot. Add the tomato mixture and scatter the olives over. Season lightly. Cover and cook on Low for 1½–2 hours or until everything is just cooked through. Taste and re-season if necessary.

3   Serve spooned over a bed of rice and sprinkled with chopped parsley.

This dish is based on a speciality from Andalusia in Spain. The people there quite often use anchovies in the sauce but I prefer the more delicate flavour of prawns. Though this dish can be pan-fried, it is very easy to burn the butter. Cooking it in the slow cooker gives a softer, melting finish, which I find superb.

poached skate wings in prawn and caper butter

SERVES 4

4 skate wings
Salt and freshly ground black pepper
50 g/2 oz/¼ cup unsalted (sweet)
    butter, cut into small pieces
60 ml/4 tbsp olive oil
1 garlic clove, crushed
30 ml/2 tbsp chopped fresh parsley
15 ml/1 tbsp chopped fresh tarragon
Juice of 1 lime

15 ml/1 tbsp salted capers, rinsed
100 g/4 oz cooked, peeled prawns
    (shrimp)
Lime wedges and sprigs of fresh
    parsley, to garnish

TO SERVE:
Crushed (not mashed) potatoes and peas

1 Lightly season the skate wings with salt and pepper.

2 Put the butter and oil in the crock pot and heat on Low for about 15 minutes until the butter has melted.

3 Slide in the skate wings and turn over in the butter. Add all the remaining ingredients and cook for 1–2 hours on Low until the skate is tender. Taste and re-season, if necessary.

4 Carefully transfer the fish and the prawn and caper butter mixture to warm plates, garnish each with lime wedges and sprigs of parsley and serve with crushed potatoes and peas.

Portuguese sardines are famous – and quite rightly. These small fish from the herring family are wonderful when charcoal-grilled but you may not have had them slowly cooked with fragrant fresh basil, sweet onions and juicy tomatoes before. Make sure you (or ask your fishmonger to) clean and scale the fish before cooking for the best results.

slow-cooked sardines with basil, onion and tomatoes

SERVES 4

8 large fresh sardines, cleaned and
    scaled
Salt and freshly ground black pepper
Juice of ½ lemon
30 ml/2 tbsp olive oil
1 large onion, halved and thinly
    sliced

4 ripe tomatoes, thinly sliced
2.5 ml/½ tsp caster (superfine) sugar
30 ml/2 tbsp chopped fresh basil
30 ml/2 tbsp chopped fresh parsley

TO SERVE:
Plain boiled potatoes and a crisp
    green salad

1   Season the fish with salt, pepper and the lemon juice. Smear half the oil in the crock pot and lay the fish on top, in a single layer if possible.

2   Heat the remaining oil in a frying pan. Add the onion and fry gently, stirring, for 2–3 minutes until fairly soft and lightly golden. Scatter the contents of the pan over the sardines.

3   Lay the tomato slices on top and sprinkle with the sugar, a little more salt and pepper, the basil and the parsley. Cover and cook on Low for 1½–2 hours until the tomatoes are soft and the fish is cooked through.

4   Carefully transfer the fish and tomatoes to warm plates. Serve with plain boiled potatoes and a crisp green salad.

Cooking fish in sparkling wine is popular in many countries but I believe it originated in France with Champagne. You can use a less expensive sparkling wine if you think the real thing is too decadent! Whichever you choose, the end result is a delicately flavoured dish that oozes elegance. Serve the rest of the bottle chilled with the fish.

salmon poached in champagne

SERVES 4

4 thick salmon steaks
150 ml/¼ pint/⅔ cup Champagne
15 ml/1 tbsp cognac
60 ml/4 tbsp water
1 bay leaf
6 black peppercorns
1 slice of onion
50 g/2 oz/¼ cup butter, cut into small pieces

75 ml/5 tbsp double (heavy) cream
Salt and white pepper
12 chive stalks, to garnish

TO SERVE:
Steamed potatoes sprinkled with chopped parsley, and mangetout (snow peas)

1 Put the fish in the crock pot.

2 Place the Champagne, cognac, water, bay leaf, peppercorns and onion in a saucepan. Bring to the boil, then pour over the salmon. Cover and cook on Low for 1 hour.

3 Carefully pour off the cooking liquid into a saucepan. Leave the fish in the crock pot on Low. Discard the bay leaf, peppercorns and onion slice. Boil the liquid rapidly until well reduced and syrupy.

4 Whisk in the butter a piece at a time until slightly thickened, then whisk in the cream and season to taste.

5 Carefully transfer the fish to warm plates, spoon the sauce over and garnish each with three chive stalks, laid attractively on top in a criss-cross pattern. Serve with steamed potatoes sprinkled with chopped parsley and mangetout.

This is my version of a delicious Egyptian dish, which sometimes uses
chick peas instead of lentils. The main principle is that the rice dish is
cooked with the spices and tomatoes to form a lovely flavoursome pilaf,
then the prawns are quickly sautéed and thrown on at the last moment.
The cucumber and yoghurt makes a lovely, fresh accompaniment.

lentil pilaf with sautéed
lemon prawns

SERVES 4

175 g/6 oz/1 cup green or brown
  lentils, soaked in cold water for
  several hours or overnight
60 ml/4 tbsp olive oil
1 onion, finely chopped
2 large garlic cloves, crushed
5 ml/1 tsp crushed dried chillies
5 ml/1 tsp ground cumin
2 cardamom pods, split
225 g/8 oz/1 cup risotto rice
4 tomatoes, skinned and chopped
450 ml/¾ pint/2 cups boiling
  chicken or fish stock
Salt and freshly ground black pepper

400 g/14 oz raw shelled king prawns
  (jumbo shrimp) with the tails on,
  thawed if frozen
25 g/1 oz/2 tbsp unsalted (sweet)
  butter
Finely grated zest and juice of
  1 lemon
30 ml/2 tbsp roughly chopped fresh
  dill (dill weed)

TO SERVE:
Thinly sliced cucumber dressed with
  plain yoghurt

1 Drain the lentils. Place in the crock pot and cover with plenty of
boiling water. Cook on High for 2 hours until soft. Turn off the slow
cooker. Remove the pot from the base and drain off any excess
liquid.

2 Meanwhile, heat half the oil in a frying pan, add the onion and
garlic and fry, stirring, for 3–4 minutes until lightly golden. Stir in
the spices and rice and stir until the grains of rice are glistening
with the oil.

3 Add to the cooked lentils with the tomatoes, stock and some salt
and pepper. Cover and cook on Low for 1½ hours until the rice is
cooked but still has some texture and the liquid has been absorbed.

4 Meanwhile, run the point of a sharp knife down the back of each
prawn and remove the black vein.

5 Just before the rice is cooked, heat the remaining oil with the butter in a clean frying pan. Add the prawns and toss quickly until pink all over. Add the lemon zest and juice and a little seasoning.

6 Spoon the rice and lentil mixture into bowls. Add the prawns and their juices and sprinkle with the dill. Serve with thinly sliced cucumber dressed with yoghurt.

You can buy squid rings already prepared, which saves a lot of time and effort. Sadly, perhaps because they have been frozen before they reach the fishmonger, they can be lacking in flavour but cooking them with garlic, peppers, chilli flakes and lots of herbs makes them taste absolutely fabulous!

stewed squid rings with peppers and chilli flakes

SERVES 4

900 g/2 lb prepared squid rings
2 red (bell) peppers, finely chopped
1 green pepper, finely chopped
1 onion, very finely chopped
3 garlic cloves, crushed
90 ml/6 tbsp olive oil
2.5 ml/½ tsp crushed dried chillies
Juice of 1 large lemon

Salt and freshly ground black pepper
30 ml/2 tbsp chopped fresh parsley
30 ml/2 tbsp chopped fresh thyme
Lemon wedges and sprigs of fresh
    parsley, to garnish

TO SERVE:
Crusty bread and a green salad,
    including some sliced avocado

1 Put all the ingredients except the chopped herbs in the crock pot and toss well. Cover and cook on Low for 2 hours until the squid is tender. Taste and re-season, if necessary.

2 Switch off the slow cooker, throw in the herbs and stir gently. Re-cover and leave to stand for 5 minutes to allow the flavours to develop.

3 Serve in bowls garnished with lemon wedges and sprigs of parsley, with crusty bread and a green salad.

A Spanish friend of mine gave me her version of this dish many years ago. It actually originated in Galicia, which is in north-western Spain rather than on the Mediterranean, but you will find similar dishes throughout the country. You can use other meaty fish such as cod or haddock, if you prefer.

braised hake with potatoes, beans and red peppers

SERVES 4

900 g/2 lb potatoes, cut into walnut-sized chunks
100 g/4 oz thin green beans, topped, tailed and halved
75 ml/5 tbsp olive oil
2 large onions, thinly sliced
2 garlic cloves, crushed
2 red (bell) peppers, roughly diced

60 ml/4 tbsp water
5 ml/1 tsp pimentón
Salt and freshly ground black pepper
4 pieces of hake fillet, about 150 g/5 oz each
45 ml/3 tbsp chopped fresh parsley
Lemon wedges, to garnish

1 Parboil the potatoes and beans in lightly salted water for 2 minutes. Drain and tip into the crock pot.

2 Heat the oil in a frying pan, add the onions, garlic and peppers and fry gently, stirring, for 2 minutes until softened but not browned. Add the water, pimentón and some salt and pepper and tip into the crock pot. Toss with the potatoes and beans. Cover and cook on High for 2 hours until just tender. Turn down the slow cooker to Low.

3 Lay the fish on top, season lightly, re-cover and cook on Low for 1 hour until the fish is tender. Transfer to warm plates, scatter the parsley over and garnish with lemon wedges.

VEGETARIAN
MAIN MEALS

With such an abundance of fabulous vegetables, it's no wonder there are so many delicious vegetarian dishes created throughout the region. Here I've selected my favourites for you to enjoy. Many of them are adapted from the originals, firstly for making in the slow cooker and secondly to introduce some exciting new flavours and textures. Others are my own creations from scratch, using all-Mediterranean ingredients. For a dish leaning towards the traditional, you could go for *imam bayildi* – stuffed aubergines – from Turkey; but for something a little bit different, try my Creamy Pumpkin, Sage and Barley Risotto with Dolcelatte.

This Turkish dish, called imam bayildi, *has numerous variations. I use a mixture of tomatoes, onion, olives, sultanas and pine nuts flavoured with harissa paste to fill the aubergines, then the finished dish is garnished with yoghurt, cucumber and mint. These are best served neither hot nor cold but warm.*

turkish-style aubergine slippers

SERVES 4

2 large aubergines (eggplants), trimmed and halved lengthways
90 ml/6 tbsp boiling water
4 beefsteak tomatoes
30 ml/2 tbsp pine nuts
30 ml/2 tbsp olive oil
1 onion, finely chopped
2 garlic cloves, crushed
5 ml/1 tsp harissa paste
15 ml/1 tbsp tomato purée (paste)
60 ml/4 tbsp cold water
A good pinch of caster (superfine) sugar
30 ml/2 tbsp sliced stoned (pitted) black olives

30 ml/2 tbsp sultanas (golden raisins)
Salt and freshly ground black pepper
120 ml/4 fl oz/½ cup thick plain yoghurt
30 ml/2 tbsp chopped fresh mint
5 cm/2 in piece of cucumber, coarsely grated
30 ml/2 tbsp chopped fresh parsley, to garnish

TO SERVE:
Warm pitta breads and a green salad

1 Score the aubergine flesh in a small criss-cross pattern, cutting deep into the flesh but taking care not to cut through the skin. Place in the crock pot and pour the boiling water around. Cover and cook on High for 1 hour until the flesh is fairly tender.

2 Meanwhile, chop three of the tomatoes and thinly slice the fourth.

3 Heat a frying pan, add the pine nuts and fry quickly to brown. Tip out of the pan immediately so they don't burn and set aside.

4 Heat the oil in the pan, add the onion and garlic and fry for 2 minutes, stirring, to soften. Add the chopped tomatoes, harissa paste, tomato purée, water, sugar, olives, sultanas and pine nuts. Cook for 2 minutes, stirring, to soften the tomatoes. Season to taste.

5 Using a spoon, gently press down the cooked pulp in each of the aubergine halves to form a shell. Spoon in the tomato mixture and top with the tomato slices. Re-cover and cook on High for a further 1–2 hours until cooked through.

6 Remove the crock pot from the base and leave the aubergines to cool until warm.

7 Meanwhile, mix the yoghurt with the mint. Squeeze the cucumber thoroughly to remove excess moisture and stir in. Season to taste.

8 Carefully transfer the aubergines to serving plates and spoon the juices over. Sprinkle with the parsley. Put a large spoonful of the cucumber yoghurt to one side and serve with warm pitta breads and a green salad.

This Middle Eastern casserole is not only rich and tasty but also highly nutritious. It uses very little fat but is packed with vegetables, fruits and pulses. I like to serve it just with some Mediterranean flat breads and a salad but you could serve rice or couscous too, if you like. Use two large cans of chick peas if you prefer and start at Step 2.

middle eastern
chick pea tagine

SERVES 4

225 g/8 oz/1¼ cups dried chick peas (garbanzos), soaked in cold water for several hours or overnight
15 ml/1 tbsp olive oil
2 onions, chopped
2 garlic cloves, crushed
2 celery sticks, chopped
2 carrots, diced
5 ml/1 tsp ground cumin
2.5 ml/½ tsp ground cinnamon
A good pinch of ground cloves

2 courgettes (zucchini), sliced
100 g/4 oz whole button mushrooms
400 g/14 oz/large can of chopped tomatoes
75 g/3 oz/½ cup prunes, stoned (pitted) and quartered
15 ml/1 tbsp tomato purée (paste)
1 bay leaf
Salt and freshly ground black pepper
A few torn coriander (cilantro) leaves, to garnish

1 Drain the chick peas, place in a saucepan and just cover with fresh water. Bring to the boil and boil rapidly for 10 minutes. Tip into the crock pot and cook on High for 3–4 hours until tender.

2 Meanwhile, heat the oil in a saucepan, add the onions, garlic, celery and carrots and fry for 2 minutes, stirring. Add the spices and stir for 1 minute. Tip into the crock pot, then stir in all the remaining ingredients, seasoning well. Cover and cook on High for 2–3 hours until the vegetables are tender and everything is bathed in a rich sauce.

3 Discard the bay leaf, taste and re-season, if necessary. Spoon into bowls, garnish with the coriander and serve hot.

This is a stunning mixture of flavours and textures that will delight even ardent meat eaters. The soft, orange pumpkin, the nutty barley, the fragrant sage and the creamy yet salty Dolcelatte merge together to form a glorious combination. Barley makes a particularly good risotto in the slow cooker as it doesn't become too soft.

creamy pumpkin, sage and barley risotto with dolcelatte

SERVES 4

30 ml/2 tbsp olive oil
1 onion, chopped
1 garlic clove, crushed
450 g/1 lb pumpkin, diced
350 g/12 oz/generous 1⅔ cups pearl barley
900 ml/1½ pints/3¾ cups boiling vegetable stock made with 2 stock cubes

Salt and freshly ground black pepper
30 ml/2 tbsp chopped fresh sage
100 g/4 oz/1 cup crumbled Dolcelatte cheese
45 ml/3 tbsp double (heavy) cream

TO SERVE:
Ciabatta bread and a mixed salad

1 Heat the oil in a frying pan. Add the onion, garlic and pumpkin and fry for 2 minutes, stirring, until softened but not browned. Stir in the barley until glistening, then tip into the crock pot.

2 Add the stock, some salt and pepper and half the sage. Stir well, cover and cook on High for 2–3 hours until the barley and pumpkin are tender. Turn off the slow cooker.

3 Gently stir in the Dolcelatte and cream. Cover and leave for 5 minutes.

4 Spoon into warm bowls and sprinkle with the remaining sage. Serve with ciabatta bread and a mixed salad.

Champignons à la Grecque has numerous variations. This is my favourite as I love the addition of coarsely crushed coriander seeds, but you can omit them if you're not keen on their fragrance. The dish is equally delicious chilled and served as a salad with crusty bread or a rice salad. You can also serve it as a starter in smaller quantities or as part of a buffet.

mushrooms with white wine, coriander seeds and tomatoes

SERVES 4

450 g/1 lb baby button mushrooms
  (or larger ones, quartered)
1 bouquet garni sachet
5 ml/1 tsp coriander (cilantro)
  seeds, coarsely crushed
90 ml/6 tbsp olive oil
1 large onion, finely chopped
1 garlic clove, crushed
175 ml/6 fl oz/¾ cup dry white wine

4 tomatoes, skinned and chopped
A good pinch of caster (superfine)
  sugar
Salt and freshly ground black pepper
30 ml/2 tbsp chopped fresh parsley,
  to garnish

TO SERVE:
Wild rice mix

1   Wipe the mushrooms and trim the stalks but leave the mushrooms whole. Place in the crock pot and add the bouquet garni and coriander seeds.

2   Heat half of the oil in a frying pan, add the onion and garlic and fry gently for 2 minutes, stirring, until softened but not browned.

3   Add the wine and tomatoes to the pan, bring to the boil and pour over the mushrooms. Add the sugar and some salt and pepper. Cover and cook on High for 2–3 hours.

4   Taste and re-season, if necessary, then discard the bouquet garni. Remove the crock pot from its base and leave the mushrooms to stand for 15 minutes to cool slightly. Spoon over wild rice mix in bowls, trickle the remaining oil over and sprinkle with the parsley before serving.

This is more fusion food than genuine Mediterranean but it uses true Italian flavours to create a delicious light lunch or supper dish. You can ring the changes by adding a few chopped stoned olives or some sliced mushrooms. For a more substantial meal, serve the squash with some tomato noodles (see the recipe on page 54).

cheese-topped acorn squash with sage and sun-blushed tomatoes

SERVES 4

2 acorn squashes
4 sun-blushed tomatoes, chopped
100 g/4 oz/½ cup Ricotta cheese
1 garlic clove, crushed
15 ml/1 tbsp chopped fresh parsley
15 ml/1 tbsp chopped fresh sage
1 large egg
60 ml/4 tbsp milk

60 ml/4 tbsp freshly grated
   Parmesan cheese
Salt and freshly ground black pepper
Small sprigs of fresh sage, to
   garnish

TO SERVE:
Crusty bread and a mixed salad

1 Halve the squashes and scoop out and discard the seeds. Place in the crock pot with about 2.5 cm/1 in of boiling water surrounding them. Cover and cook on High for 1–2 hours until just tender.

2 Blot the cavities in the squashes with kitchen paper (paper towels) to remove excess moisture. Turn down the slow cooker to Low.

3 Divide the tomatoes between the cavities. Beat together all the remaining ingredients except half the Parmesan, seasoning to taste. Spoon the mixture into the cavities in the squash. Cover and cook on Low for 1 hour until the custard has set.

4 Transfer to plates, sprinkle with the remaining Parmesan and garnish each with small sprigs of sage. Serve with crusty bread and a mixed salad.

This Spanish dish, tumbet, *is popular in the Balearic Islands – particularly on Majorca. There it is often cooked in a terracotta casserole dish and baked slowly in the oven. Here I've adapted it for the slow cooker and, to save preparation time, I've used canned tomatoes to make the sauce. The eggs are my idea!*

spanish aubergine, pepper and potato stew

SERVES 4

Olive oil
2 onions, chopped
2 garlic cloves, crushed
2 × 400 g/14 oz/large cans of
  chopped tomatoes
30 ml/2 tbsp tomato purée (paste)
5 ml/1 tsp dried marjoram
A good pinch of caster (superfine)
  sugar
Salt and freshly ground black pepper

4 potatoes, scrubbed and sliced
2 large aubergines (eggplants),
  sliced
4 red (bell) peppers, cut into
  thickish strips
4 large eggs

TO SERVE:
Olives, crusty bread and a crisp
green salad

1 Heat 30 ml/2 tbsp of the oil in a saucepan, add the onions and garlic and fry for 3 minutes, stirring, until softened and lightly golden. Add the tomatoes, tomato purée, marjoram, sugar and some salt and pepper and simmer, stirring, for 5 minutes until thick and pulpy.

2 Heat enough oil to cover the base of a large frying pan and fry the potatoes, then the aubergines until golden, adding more oil as necessary. Drain well on kitchen paper (paper towels).

3 Heat 30 ml/2 tbsp more oil, add the peppers and fry for about 3 minutes until softened.

4 Put the potatoes in the crock pot in an even layer. Add a third of the tomato sauce and spread it out. Top with the aubergines, then half the remaining sauce. Add the peppers, then the remaining sauce. Cover and cook on High for 2 hours.

5 Remove the pot from the base and leave to cool slightly (this dish is best served just above room temperature).

6 Meanwhile, put the eggs in a pan of cold water. Bring to the boil and boil for 4 minutes only (if using medium eggs, cook for 3½ minutes), then plunge immediately into cold water to prevent further cooking. Carefully remove the shells.

7 Spoon the cooked stew on to warm plates. Top each with an egg and carefully cut it almost in half so the yolk runs out slightly. Serve with a dish of olives, some crusty bread and a crisp green salad.

There are versions of this called chakchouka *in the Middle East and* huevos a la flamenca *in Spain.* Piperade *is another similar dish from France, but the eggs are scrambled rather than cooked whole and usually only sweet peppers are used. The Spanish version is often served with the addition of chorizo sausage.*

sweet and hot peppers
with onions and eggs

SERVES 4

60 ml/4 tbsp olive oil
2 large onions, thinly sliced
2 garlic cloves, crushed
3 red (bell) peppers, thinly sliced
1–2 large red chillies, seeded and
   thinly sliced
700 g/1½ lb ripe tomatoes, skinned
   and chopped

2.5 ml/½ tsp caster (superfine) sugar
Salt and freshly ground black pepper
100 g/4 oz/1 cup frozen peas,
   thawed (optional)
4 eggs

TO SERVE:
Crusty bread

1 Heat the oil in a frying pan, add the onions and garlic and fry for 2 minutes, stirring. Tip into the crock pot and add all the remaining ingredients except the eggs. Stir well.

2 Cover and cook on High for 2 hours until the vegetables are tender. Taste and re-season, if necessary. Turn down the slow cooker to Low.

3 Make four wells in the mixture and break an egg into each. Cover and cook for 10–15 minutes until the eggs are cooked to your liking. Serve straight away with crusty bread.

You'll find versions of this dish all over Greece. Fasoles karavisies literally means 'beans as cooked on a boat'. I like the added interest of celery and carrot in the tomato sauce but you'll sometimes find it with the beans simply cooked with tomato juice and onion. You could use three drained large cans of butter beans and start at Step 2.

butter beans
bathed in tomato sauce

SERVES 4

350 g/12 oz/2 cups butter (lima) beans, soaked in cold water for several hours or overnight
45 ml/3 tbsp olive oil, plus extra for serving
2 onions, finely chopped
2 garlic cloves, crushed
1 large carrot, finely chopped
2 celery sticks, finely chopped

300 ml/½ pint/1¼ cups tomato juice
15 ml/1 tbsp tomato purée (paste)
5 ml/1 tsp dried oregano
1.5 ml/¼ tsp crushed dried chillies
Salt and freshly ground black pepper
45 ml/3 tbsp chopped fresh parsley

TO SERVE:
Fresh crusty bread, spring onions (scallions) and radishes

1   Drain the beans and place in a saucepan of fresh water. Bring to the boil and boil rapidly for 10 minutes. Reduce the heat and simmer for 45 minutes until almost cooked. Drain and place in the crock pot.

2   Meanwhile, heat the oil in a pan, add the prepared vegetables and fry for 2 minutes, stirring, until softened but not browned. Add all the remaining ingredients except half the parsley and bring to the boil. Add to the beans, stir, cover and cook on High for 2–3 hours until tender and bathed in a rich sauce.

3   Stir, taste and re-season, if necessary. Serve in bowls, trickled with olive oil and sprinkled with the remaining parsley, with fresh crusty bread and dishes of spring onions and radishes.

This is a classic that needs little introduction – the plus is that it is ideal for making in the slow cooker. In the old days you had to boil the pasta before you started but now, with the benefit of no-need-to-precook varieties, this dish takes very little time to prepare and will cook in just a few hours.

spinach and ricotta cannelloni with tomato and basil sauce

SERVES 4

25 g/1 oz/2 tbsp butter, melted
100 ml/3½ fl oz/scant ½ cup boiling water
450 g/1 lb frozen chopped spinach, thawed
250 g/9 oz/generous 1 cup Ricotta cheese
2 large eggs, beaten
100 g/4 oz/1 cup grated Parmesan cheese
1.5 ml/¼ tsp grated nutmeg
Salt and freshly ground black pepper
12–16 no-need-to-precook cannelloni tubes

FOR THE SAUCE:
450 ml/¾ pint/2 cups passata (sieved tomatoes)
1 large garlic clove, crushed
2.5 ml/½ tsp clear honey
100 ml/3½ fl oz/scant ½ cup boiling water
15 ml/1 tbsp chopped fresh basil, plus a few torn leaves for garnishing

TO SERVE:
Garlic bread and a mixed salad

1   Brush half the butter over the base and just a little way up the side of the crock pot. Add half the water.

2   Squeeze the spinach well to remove all the excess moisture. Place in a bowl and mix with the Ricotta, the remaining butter, the eggs, half the Parmesan and the nutmeg. Season well.

3   Put the mixture in a piping bag fitted with a large plain tube and pipe the mixture into the cannelloni tubes. Lay them evenly in the crock pot.

4   Mix together all the sauce ingredients and pour over the pasta. Cook on High for 1½–2½ hours until the pasta is tender. Sprinkle with the remaining Parmesan, scatter a few torn basil leaves over and serve hot with garlic bread and a mixed salad.

This has lovely Middle Eastern flavours and is also colourful and nutritious! I like it served with some well-chilled thick creamy yoghurt spooned over and Mediterranean flat breads as an accompaniment. The harissa paste is not essential but it does add a richness that really enhances the dish.

tunisian sweet potato, carrot and pea casserole

SERVES 4

30 ml/2 tbsp olive oil
2 onions, chopped
2 garlic cloves, crushed
5 ml/1 tsp ground cinnamon
1.5 ml/¼ tsp crushed dried chillies
15 ml/1 tbsp clear honey
30 ml/2 tbsp lemon juice
90 ml/6 tbsp water
5 ml/1 tsp harissa paste

2 large sweet potatoes, cut into
 2 cm/¾ in dice
4 large carrots, halved and cut into
 chunks
Salt and freshly ground black pepper
225 g/8 oz/2 cups frozen peas,
 thawed
30 ml/2 tbsp chopped fresh parsley

1 Heat the oil in a frying pan, add the onions and garlic and fry for 2 minutes, stirring. Stir in the spices, honey, lemon juice, water and harissa paste and bring to the boil, stirring.

2 Put the sweet potatoes and carrots in the crock pot. Season with salt and pepper and pour the sauce over. Cover and cook on High for 2 hours until the vegetables are tender and bathed in a rich sauce.

3 Add the peas and cook for a further 30–60 minutes. Taste and re-season, if necessary. Serve sprinkled with the chopped parsley.

SIDE DISHES

When you're planning a meal with some plain grilled or fried meat, chicken or fish, you will need something tasty and moist to accompany it. Here is a selection of side dishes that will fit the bill. Whether you need a simple rice or pasta dish or a lovely saucy vegetable, they will all cook to perfection in the crock pot. One word of warning, though: pasta and rice don't sit well so make sure you're ready to eat as soon as they are cooked.

Ratatouille is perfect cooked in the slow cooker to serve hot or cold as a starter or as a side dish with chops or chicken. To turn it into a main meal, when cooked, turn the cooker down to Low, make four wells in the mixture, break an egg into each, cover and cook for a further 10–15 minutes until the eggs are cooked to your liking.

mediterranean vegetables with herbs and garlic

SERVES 4

30 ml/2 tbsp olive oil
1 red onion, sliced
1 aubergine (eggplant), sliced
1 red (bell) pepper, sliced
1 green pepper, sliced
2 courgettes (zucchini), sliced
1 garlic clove, crushed
2 beefsteak tomatoes, skinned and chopped

15 ml/1 tbsp tomato purée (paste)
90 ml/6 tbsp red or dry white wine
5 ml/1 tsp clear honey
Salt and freshly ground black pepper
5 ml/1 tsp chopped fresh or
    1.5 ml/¼ tsp dried thyme
15 ml/1 tbsp chopped fresh basil
15 ml/1 tbsp chopped fresh parsley

1   Heat the oil in a frying pan, add the onion and fry for 2 minutes, stirring. Tip into the crock pot. Add all the remaining vegetables and toss with the hands to coat in the oil.

2   Blend the tomato purée with the wine and honey. Add to the pot with some salt, pepper and the thyme. Cover and cook on High for 2–3 hours until the vegetables are soft but still have a little texture.

3   Taste and re-season, if necessary. Stir in the basil and parsley and serve.

Risotto milanese *needs to be eaten as soon as it is ready or it will become stodgy. If this should happen, stir a little extra single cream into it just before you dish it up. It is lovely as a starter for six or as an accompaniment to meat, chicken or fish. If you like, add some dry-fried lardons to the ingredients before cooking.*

creamy saffron rice
with parmesan

SERVES 4

30 ml/2 tbsp olive oil
1 onion, finely chopped
350 g/12 oz/1½ cups risotto rice
A good pinch of saffron strands
750 ml/1¼ pints/3 cups boiling
   chicken stock
Salt and freshly ground black pepper

25 g/1 oz/2 tbsp unsalted (sweet)
   butter
60 ml/4 tbsp single (light) cream
15 g/½ oz/2 tbsp freshly grated
   Parmesan cheese
15 ml/1 tbsp chopped fresh parsley

1   Heat the oil in a frying pan, add the onion and fry for 2 minutes to soften. Tip into the crock pot.

2   Rinse the rice well and drain. Add to the onion and stir until every grain is coated in the oil.

3   Add the saffron and stock to the pot and season lightly. Cover and cook on Low for 1½ hours until the rice has absorbed most of the liquid but still has some 'bite'. Remove the pot from the cooker.

4   Stir in the butter until melted, then the cream and Parmesan. Serve straight away, sprinkled with the parsley.

This is the perfect basic accompaniment to any plain fish, chicken or grilled meat. It is also lovely smothered in grated Cheddar or Mozzarella cheese as a light lunch or supper dish. Don't use quick-cook macaroni or the end result will be far too stodgy. It is important to have plenty of sauce so I've used canned tomatoes.

macaroni in tomato and mascarpone sauce

SERVES 4

15 ml/1 tbsp olive oil
1 onion, finely chopped
1 garlic clove, crushed
400 g/14 oz/large can of chopped
    tomatoes
90 ml/6 tbsp red wine
150 ml/¼ pint/⅔ cup boiling water
30 ml/2 tbsp tomato purée (paste)

2.5 ml/½ tsp caster (superfine) sugar
2.5 ml/½ tsp dried basil
175 g/6 oz short-cut macaroni
Salt and freshly ground black pepper
100 g/4 oz/½ cup Mascarpone
    cheese
30 ml/2 tbsp freshly grated
    Parmesan cheese

1 Heat the oil in a frying pan, add the onion and garlic and fry for 2 minutes to soften. Tip into the crock pot.

2 Add the chopped tomatoes, wine, water, tomato purée, sugar and basil to the pan and bring to the boil. Tip into the crock pot and stir in the macaroni and some salt and pepper.

3 Cover and cook on High for 2 hours until the pasta is tender and has absorbed most of the liquid but is bathed in sauce. Taste and re-season, if necessary. Stir in the Mascarpone and serve dusted with the Parmesan.

This is based on the classic French dish pommes dauphinoise, *of which I have created numerous versions over the years. Here the potatoes are layered with garlic and double cream for slow-cooking. At the end they're topped with a crisp buttery crumb and herb crust mixed with Gruyère cheese. You can cook this directly in a small round crock pot.*

creamy potatoes with garlic and a herb crumb crust

SERVES 4

Butter for greasing
450 g/1 lb potatoes, peeled and
   thinly sliced
2 garlic cloves, crushed
Salt and freshly ground black pepper
284 ml/8 fl oz carton of double
   (heavy) cream

FOR THE CRUST:
25 g/1 oz/2 tbsp butter
50 g/2 oz/1 cup fresh breadcrumbs
30 ml/2 tbsp chopped fresh parsley
5 ml/1 tsp dried herbes de Provence
50 g/2 oz/½ cup finely grated
   Gruyère (Swiss) cheese

1 Grease a 1.2 litre/2 pint/5 cup heatproof dish that will fit in the crock pot with a little butter. Layer the potatoes in the dish with the garlic and some salt and pepper. Pour the cream over. Cover the dish with foil, twisting and folding under the rim to secure.

2 Place in the crock pot with enough boiling water to come half way up the side of the dish. Cover and cook on High for 3–4 hours until the potatoes are tender.

3 When the potatoes are nearly ready, to make the crust, melt the butter in a frying pan. Add the breadcrumbs and fry, tossing, until crisp and golden. Toss in the herbs and Gruyère and add a little salt and pepper. Scatter over the potatoes and serve straight away.

Patatas a lo pobre, *or poor man's potatoes, is a popular southern Spanish dish. As always, there are numerous variations, some with peppers added, others with little bits of fatty pork belly or chorizo. I like this plainer version that is great as a tapas or served to accompany grilled pork chops or chicken portions.*

potatoes with caramelised onions and sherry vinegar

90 ml/6 tbsp olive oil
25 g/1 oz/2 tbsp butter
2 large onions, thinly sliced
5 ml/1 tsp caster (superfine) sugar
30 ml/2 tbsp sherry vinegar

4 large potatoes, peeled and thinly sliced
Salt and freshly ground black pepper
2 large garlic cloves, very finely chopped
30 ml/2 tbsp chopped fresh parsley

1 Heat 15 ml/1 tbsp of the oil and the butter in a frying pan. Add the onions and fry for about 3 minutes, stirring, until softened. Add the sugar and sherry vinegar and stir over a high heat for 5 minutes until richly golden.

2 Tip into the crock pot and add the potatoes. Mix well, making sure the slices of potato are separated.

3 Heat the remaining oil in the pan and tip into the crock pot. Toss again. Season well, cover and cook on High for 2–3 hours until the potatoes are really tender. Switch off the slow cooker.

4 Mix together the garlic and parsley and sprinkle over the potatoes. Re-cover and leave to stand for 5 minutes. Serve hot.

This French-style recipe brings out the full flavour of the peas and makes the perfect accompaniment to any meat or fish. However, I like it best with lightly sautéed lamb cutlets and some baby new potatoes – a perfect, simple meal that is also elegant enough for a special occasion.

creamed peas with lettuce and baby onions

SERVES 4

15 g/½ oz/1 tbsp butter, cut into small pieces
12 button (pearl) onions, peeled but left whole
120 ml/4 fl oz/½ cup boiling chicken or vegetable stock
15 ml/1 tbsp cornflour (cornstarch)

15 ml/1 tbsp water
350 g/12 oz/3 cups frozen peas, thawed
1 round lettuce, finely shredded
5 ml/1 tsp dried mint
60 ml/4 tbsp double (heavy) cream
Salt and freshly ground black pepper

1 Put the butter, onions and stock in the crock pot. Cover and cook on High for 1 hour.

2 Blend the cornflour with the water and stir into the pot, then add the peas, lettuce and mint. Re-cover and cook for a further 1 hour.

3 Stir in the cream and season to taste. Serve hot.

There are versions of this all over Europe. This Italian one is called cavolo
rosso con mele. *Some cooks don't add spices; others omit the raisins. I like
the combination of the two. You can use cooking apples if you want a
more tart end result but I prefer the sweetness of the fruit with the acidity
of the vinegar.*

braised red cabbage
with apples

SERVES 6–8

1 small red cabbage, shredded
1 onion, thinly sliced
2 eating (dessert) apples, thinly
   sliced
A large handful of raisins
2 cloves

5 cm/2 in piece of cinnamon stick
Salt and freshly ground black pepper
30 ml/2 tbsp light brown sugar
30 ml/2 tbsp red wine vinegar
45 ml/3 tbsp boiling water

1 Mix the cabbage with the onion, apples and raisins, the spices,
some salt and pepper and the sugar in the crock pot.

2 Mix together the wine vinegar and water and pour over. Cover
and cook on High for 2–3 hours until tender. Discard the spices,
stir and serve.

This is based on a recipe from Liguria, the small coastal region of north-western Italy. I have adapted it for the slow cooker as I find it brings out the wonderful flavour of the mushrooms. The addition of the cream is my idea as it gives a lovely saucy end result but, for a more traditional feel, you could omit it altogether.

mixed mushrooms
with garlic and potatoes

SERVES 4

30 ml/2 tbsp olive oil
350 g/12 oz mixed wild and
   cultivated mushrooms, chopped
   or sliced
2 garlic cloves, crushed
Salt and freshly ground black pepper

4 potatoes, peeled and thinly sliced
150 ml/¼ pint/⅔ cup single (light)
   cream
15 g/½ oz/1 tbsp butter
A small handful of torn basil leaves

1   Grease the crock pot with a little of the oil. Heat the remainder in a saucepan and add the mushrooms and garlic. Season and cook gently for 2 minutes, stirring.

2   Add a layer of half the potatoes to the crock pot, then all the mushrooms, then the remaining potatoes. Season the top, then pour the cream over and dot with the butter.

3   Cover and cook on High for 3–4 hours until really tender. Switch off the slow cooker. Scatter the basil over the potatoes, re-cover and leave to stand for 5 minutes. Serve straight from the dish.

This is another Italian speciality, which can also be made with turnip instead of beetroot and radicchio instead of chicory. I like to use red chicory when I can find it. This dish is lovely as an accompaniment but is also delicious stirred through some freshly cooked pasta for a light lunch or supper.

chicory with beetroot, capers and tomatoes

SERVES 4

4 heads of chicory (Belgian endive)
1 large garlic clove, very finely
   chopped
15 ml/1 tbsp pickled capers, drained
   and chopped
2 plum tomatoes, skinned and
   chopped

1 good-sized fresh beetroot (red
   beet), peeled and grated
45 ml/3 tbsp olive oil
Salt and freshly ground black pepper
150 ml/¼ pint/⅔ cup boiling chicken
   or vegetable stock
Salt and freshly ground black pepper

1 Cut a cone shape out of the base of each head of chicory and discard. Cut each head in half lengthways. Blanch in boiling water for 2 minutes, then drain and place in a shallow dish that will fit inside the crock pot. Add about 5 mm/¼ in of boiling water to the pot.

2 Add all the remaining ingredients to the chicory. Place the dish in the crock pot, cover and cook on High for 1–2 hours until the tomatoes are soft. Taste and re-season, if necessary.

DESSERTS

You may not think desserts would be the usual things to cook in your slow cooker but they will be a revelation, I promise. Many of the recipes in this section take full advantage of the variety of succulent poaching and stewing fruits found in this region, plus smooth, creamy custards and other egg-based dishes and dairy delights such as creamy Italian rice pudding, a soft and velvety cheesecake, chocolate torte and a version of boozy tiramisu. All these desserts are not only possible – they're utterly fabulous!

This classic baked cream with a burnt sugar top can be cooked plain but I thought you might like to try it with whole large muscatel raisins, soaked in brandy, in the base of the dishes. The result is something quite magical. You can experiment with other dried fruits too, such as chopped apricots, figs or peaches. You will need a large crock pot for this recipe.

crème brûlée
with brandied raisins

SERVES 4

50 g/2 oz/⅓ cup large stoned
  (pitted) muscatel raisins
60 ml/4 tbsp brandy
2 eggs
75 g/3 oz/⅓ cup caster (superfine)
  sugar

450 ml/¾ pint/2 cups double (heavy)
  cream
5 ml/1 tsp vanilla essence (extract)

1 Separate the raisins (they tend to stick together) and place in a small bowl. Stir in the brandy and leave to soak for at least 2 hours or until the brandy has been absorbed.

2 Whisk the eggs with 25 g/1 oz/2 tbsp of the sugar, the cream and vanilla essence. Spoon the raisins into four ramekins (custard cups) and strain the cream mixture over.

3 Place the ramekins in the crock pot with enough boiling water to come half way up the sides of the dishes. Cover and cook on Low for 2–3 hours until set.

4 Remove the ramekins from the cooker, leave to cool, then chill.

5 Just before serving, sprinkle the tops liberally with the remaining sugar. Either caramelise with a blow-torch or place under a preheated grill (broiler) until the sugar has melted and is a rich brown colour.

Whole skinned peaches are gently poached in syrup with a good splash of almond-flavoured Amaretto. The slow cooker cooks them to perfection without them losing their shape. Serve with thin almond biscuits or ratafias. You can also try using nectarines or 12 large unskinned plums in place of the peaches.

poached peaches
in amaretto syrup

SERVES 4

4 large, ripe peaches
3 cloves
1 piece of cinnamon stick
600 ml/1 pint/2½ cups dry white
   wine

175 g/6 oz/¾ cup caster (superfine)
   sugar
60 ml/4 tbsp Amaretto liqueur

1 Put the peaches in a bowl. Cover with boiling water and leave to stand for 1 minute. Peel off the skins and place in a round dish that will hold them snugly. Tuck in the cloves and cinnamon stick.

2 Place the wine and sugar in a saucepan and bring to the boil. Stir in the liqueur. Pour over the peaches – it should just cover them. Stand the dish in the slow cooker with enough boiling water to come half way up the side of the dish. Cover and cook on Low for 2–3 hours until tender.

3 Remove the dish from the slow cooker and leave to cool, then chill. When ready to serve, carefully transfer the peaches to small glass serving dishes and spoon the syrup over.

*This is my cooked version of the Italian classic, tiramisu. It must
be served well chilled. I like to serve tiny cups of scalding hot espresso
coffee with it but, for an equally exciting contrast, you could enjoy it with
a well-chilled sweet sparkling wine such as Asti Spumante or the Italian
liqueur Strega.*

brandied coffee and
ricotta pudding

SERVES 4–6

150 ml/¼ pint/⅔ cup very strong
  black coffee
60 ml/4 tbsp brandy
12 sponge (lady) finger biscuits
  (cookies)
250 g/9 oz/generous 1 cup Ricotta
  cheese
45 ml/3 tbsp icing (confectioners')
  sugar

2 eggs, separated
150 ml/¼ pint/⅔ cup double (heavy)
  or whipping cream, whipped
15 ml/1 tbsp drinking chocolate
  (sweetened chocolate) powder

TO SERVE:
Pouring cream

1 Mix together the coffee and brandy. Dip the sponge fingers in the
coffee mixture and lay them in a 1.2 litre/2 pint/5 cup shallow
heatproof serving dish. Pour any remaining coffee mixture over.

2 Beat the Ricotta with the icing sugar and egg yolks. Whisk the egg
whites until stiff.

3 Fold the egg whites into the cheese mixture and spoon on top of
the sponges. Cover the dish with foil, twisting and folding under
the rim to secure, and place in the crock pot. Pour in enough
boiling water to come half way up the side of the dish, cover and
cook on Low for 2 hours until just set.

4 Remove from the crock pot and leave to cool, then spread the
whipped cream over. Chill.

5 Just before serving, dust with the drinking chocolate. Serve with
pouring cream.

This is a lovely collection of flavours and textures – the soft apples, the slightly firmer quinces, the warm mellow spices, the sweet honey and sweet, herby red vermouth. It's worth boiling the syrup at the end to thicken it and intensify the flavours. You can make this with just apples if quinces aren't available.

poached apples with quinces and honey

SERVES 4

4 eating (dessert) apples, peeled, cored and halved
2 small quinces, peeled and halved
2 star anise
1 small piece of cinnamon stick
2 cloves

120 ml/4 fl oz/⅓ cup clear honey
150 ml/¼ pint/⅔ cup red vermouth
Finely grated zest and juice of ½ lime

TO SERVE:
150 ml/¼ pint/⅔ cup Greek-style plain yoghurt

1 Place the fruit in the crock pot in an even layer. Add the spices.

2 Mix the honey with the vermouth and lime zest and juice in a saucepan. Bring to the boil and pour over the fruit.

3 Cover and cook on Low for 2–3 hours until the fruit is soft but still holds its shape, carefully turning the fruit over half way through cooking. If liked, pour the juice into a saucepan and boil rapidly until reduced and syrupy.

4 Transfer the fruit to serving plates, discarding the spices. Spoon the juice over. Put a spoonful of yoghurt to one side and serve.

This rich cheesecake is often baked in a very slow oven. The result in a slow cooker is moister, softer and beautifully pale. It looks stunning with the dark red cherries spooned over at the last minute. You could cheat and use a can of cherry pie filling but the flavour won't be as good. Use other white soft cheese if you like.

vanilla cheesecake with fresh cherries

SERVES 8–10

200 g/7 oz/small packet of digestive biscuits (graham crackers)
75 g/3 oz/⅓ cup butter, plus a little extra for greasing
700 g/1½ lb/3 cups Mascarpone cheese
225 g/8 oz/1 cup caster (superfine) sugar
2 eggs
5 ml/1 tsp vanilla essence (extract)

FOR THE CHERRY TOPPING:
30 ml/2 tbsp apple juice
10 ml/2 tsp granulated sugar
225 g/8 oz fresh cherries, halved and stoned (pitted)
5 ml/1 tsp lemon juice
5 ml/1 tsp arrowroot

TO SERVE:
Crème fraîche

1 Finely crush the biscuits (cookies) in a plastic bag with a rolling pin. Melt the butter and stir in the biscuit crumbs. Grease a 20 cm/8 in springform tin. Place the tin on a sheet of foil and press it up the sides of the tin. Press the crumb mixture into the base and a little way up the side of the prepared tin.

2 Beat the Mascarpone with the caster sugar, eggs and vanilla essence. Spoon into the tin. Cover the tin with foil, twisting and folding under the rim to secure, and place in the crock pot. Pour in enough boiling water to cover the base of the crock pot, making sure it doesn't come above the level of the foil.

3 Cover and cook on Low for 3–4 hours until just firm. Remove from the crock pot and leave to cool, then chill.

4 To make the cherry topping, put the apple juice and sugar in a saucepan. Heat gently, stirring, until the sugar dissolves. Add the cherries and bring to the boil. Reduce the heat, cover and cook gently for 5 minutes until the cherries are soft but still hold their shape.

5 Blend the lemon juice with the arrowroot and stir into the pan. Bring to the boil, stirring gently, until thickened and clear. Leave to cool.

6 When ready to serve, remove the springform tin from the cheesecake and transfer it to a serving plate. Spoon the cherries on top and serve with crème fraîche.

This is creamy and luxurious with a speckling of vanilla seeds – a little different from the usual baked rice pudding with its brown skin and gold colour from the long stint in an oven. It is gorgeous on its own but equally delicious with the poached peaches on page 111 or any fresh soft fruit. You can serve it warm or cold.

italian vanilla
rice pudding

SERVES 4

100 g/4 oz/½ cup risotto rice
500 ml/17 fl oz/2¼ cups full-cream milk
150 ml/¼ pint/⅔ cup double (heavy) cream
½ vanilla pod, split

A good pinch of salt
50–75 g/2–3 oz/¼–⅓ cup caster (superfine) sugar (according to taste)
15 g/½ oz/1 tbsp unsalted (sweet) butter

1 Put the rice in either a small round crock pot or use a 20 cm/8 in deep dish in the pot and surround with enough boiling water to come half way up the side of the dish.

2 Bring the milk and cream to the boil in a saucepan and pour over the rice. Scrape the seeds out of the vanilla pod and put the pod and seeds, the salt and sugar in the pot. Dot with the butter.

3 Cover and cook on Low for 3 hours, stirring twice, until thick and creamy. Discard the vanilla pod before serving.

Caramelised oranges are popular all over the Mediterranean. Here they have a slight Middle Eastern flavour with the addition of dates, cinnamon and pomegranate seeds. Gently cooking the fruit rather than just macerating it brings out the intense flavour and makes this a truly memorable dessert.

caramelised oranges
with dates and pomegranate

SERVES 4

100 g/4 oz/½ cup granulated sugar
120 ml/4 fl oz/½ cup hot water
15 ml/1 tbsp orange flower water
6 oranges
100 g/4 oz fresh dates, stoned
  (pitted) and sliced

1 piece of cinnamon stick
1 pomegranate

TO SERVE:
Thick plain yoghurt

1 Put the sugar in a small, heavy pan and heat gently until the sugar melts. Turn up the heat and cook until the sugar turns a rich golden brown. Add the water (it will spit and bubble) and continue to stir until the caramel dissolves.

2 Pour the caramel syrup into a 20 cm/8 in round heatproof serving dish. Add the orange flower water. Place in the crock pot and add enough boiling water to come half way up the side of the dish (or use a small round slow cooker and place straight in the crock pot).

3 Thinly pare the zest off one of the oranges and reserve, then peel and remove the pith from all of them. Cut the fruit into slices and place in the syrup with the dates and the cinnamon stick. Cover and cook on Low for 1–1½ hours.

4 Meanwhile, cut the pared orange zest into thin strips and boil in a small pan of water for 2 minutes. Drain, rinse with cold water and drain again.

5 Quarter the pomegranate, bend back the skin and carefully remove the juicy seeds.

6 When the fruit is cooked, discard the cinnamon stick. Scatter the pomegranate seeds and orange strips over. Serve warm with thick plain yoghurt.

This Italian dessert is cooked in a mould in the slow cooker, then turned out and topped with pile of whipped cream. A gloriously unctuous real chocolate sauce is then trickled over. You could serve it with some ratafias or sponge fingers to offset the richness and add a bit of crunch. If you don't like turning puddings out, leave it in the dish.

espresso pudding
with chocolate fondant

SERVES 6–8

A little oil for greasing
250 ml/8 fl oz/1cup espresso or
    other very strong black coffee
100 g/4 oz/½ cup caster (superfine)
    sugar
6 eggs

FOR THE FONDANT:
100 g/4 oz plain (semi-sweet)
    chocolate with 70% cocoa solids

284 ml/8 fl oz carton of double
    (heavy) cream
30 ml/2 tbsp icing (confectioners')
    sugar

TO FINISH:
300 ml/½ pint/1¼ cups double
    (heavy) or whipping cream,
    whipped

1 Lightly grease a 1 litre/1¾ pint/4¼ cup round mould.

2 Mix the espresso with the sugar and stir until dissolved. Whisk in the eggs and strain into the prepared mould.

3 Stand the dish in the crock pot with enough boiling water to come half way up the side of the dish. Cover and cook on Low for 2 hours until set.

4 Remove from the crock pot and leave to cool, then chill.

5 To make the fondant, break up the chocolate and put it in a saucepan with half the cream. Heat gently, stirring, until the chocolate melts, then stir in the rest of the cream and the icing sugar. Remove from the heat and leave to cool but don't chill.

6 When ready to serve, loosen the edge of the pudding and turn it out on to a serving dish. Pile the whipped cream on top. Using a small spoon, trickle a little of the chocolate fondant over and around the pudding. Serve the rest in a small jug.

This may not be an original dessert, but it is rich and delicious and far too good to leave out. You may have made it before but I bet you've never prepared it in a slow cooker! If you buy sweetened chestnut purée, halve the quantity of icing sugar. If you prefer, coat the torte with the ganache when on the cooling rack, then transfer it to a plate once set.

chocolate and chestnut torte

SERVES 8–10

A little oil for greasing
175 g/6 oz plain (semi-sweet) chocolate with 70% cocoa solids
100 g/4 oz/½ cup unsalted (sweet) butter
225 g/8 oz/1⅓ cups icing (confectioners') sugar, sifted
435 g/15½ oz/large can of unsweetened chestnut purée (paste)

4 eggs, separated
5 ml/1 tsp vanilla essence (extract)

FOR THE GANACHE:
100 g/4 oz plain chocolate with 70% cocoa solids
120 ml/4 fl oz/½ cup double (heavy) cream

1   Grease a 20 cm/8 in springform tin and line the base with baking parchment. Stand the tin on a sheet of foil and press it up the outsides of the tin (to protect the cake from the water).

2   Break up the chocolate and place it in a bowl. Stand the bowl in a pan of simmering water and stir until melted. Alternatively, heat briefly in the microwave.

3   Beat together the butter and icing sugar until light and fluffy. Beat in the chestnut purée, egg yolks, vanilla essence and chocolate.

4   Whisk the egg whites until stiff, then fold into the chocolate mixture with a metal spoon. Spoon into the prepared tin and level the surface. Cover the tin with foil, twisting and folding under the rim to secure. Pour about 5 mm/¼ in of boiling water into the crock pot to cover the base and stand the torte in the pot. Cook on Low for 4–5 hours until fairly firm.

5   Remove from the crock pot and leave to cool in the tin.

6 To make the ganache, break up the chocolate and place in a saucepan with the cream. Heat gently, stirring all the time with a wooden spoon, until thick. Leave to cool slightly until it has a thick, coating consistency.

7 Transfer the torte to a serving plate. Spoon the ganache over, spreading it out with a palette knife so it coats the top and sides of the torte completely. Wipe the edge of the plate to clean up any excess chocolate. Leave to set but do not chill or the ganache will lose its shine.

Fresh figs are wonderful in Italy – rich and sweet. They can be grown in northern Europe too but they often lack the flavour. However, cooked with a filling of raisins and soft Mascarpone cheese and bathed in honey and Marsala, they are a treat indeed. I like to serve them with a spoonful of crème fraîche but you may prefer extra Mascarpone cheese.

figs with mascarpone and marsala

SERVES 4

8 fresh figs
50 g/2 oz/⅓ cup stoned (pitted)
    raisins, chopped
60 ml/4 tbsp clear honey
Grated zest of 1 lime

100 g/4 oz/½ cup Mascarpone
    cheese
60 ml/4 tbsp Marsala

TO SERVE:
Crème fraîche

1 Trim the bases of the figs so they will stand upright. Cut a deep cross in the top of each and squeeze gently so they open up. Arrange in the crock pot.

2 Mix together the raisins, half the honey, the lime zest and the Mascarpone and spoon into the figs. Pour the Marsala around.

3 Cover and cook on Low for 1½–2 hours until the figs are soft and the cheese has melted.

4 Transfer to shallow serving dishes and spoon the juices around. Trickle the remaining honey over and put a spoonful of crème fraîche to one side.

You wouldn't normally think of cooking meringues in a slow cooker but they work a dream! This recipe is based on a popular French dessert but is my own, very simple version that should please fruit and nut lovers alike. Raspberries are the perfect partner for the sweet nutty meringue but you could use sliced fresh peaches instead.

hazelnut meringues
with raspberries

SERVES 4

1 egg white
50 g/2 oz/¼ cup light brown sugar
40 g/1½ oz/⅓ cup ground hazelnuts
   (filberts)
1.5 ml/¼ tsp vanilla essence
   (extract)

150 ml/¼ pint/⅔ cup double (heavy)
   or whipping cream
225 g/8 oz fresh raspberries
15 ml/1 tbsp icing (confectioners')
   sugar, sifted

1 Whisk the egg white until stiff. Whisk in half the sugar and whisk until stiff and glossy. Whisk in the remaining sugar. Fold in the hazelnuts and vanilla essence.

2 Line the base of a large crock pot with non-stick baking parchment. Spread the meringue in four small ovals in the base of the pot, hollowing out the centres to form 'nests'. Cover and cook on Low for 2–2½ hours until the meringues are a good biscuit colour and fairly crisp. Turn off the heat and leave the meringues in it until they are cold and crisp.

3 Transfer the meringues to small plates. Whip the cream until peaking and spoon into the nests. Pile the raspberries on top and dust with sifted icing sugar.

Petits pots au chocolat *are little cups of pure heaven for chocoholics but are very rich. I like to cook them in small coffee cups and serve them on the saucers with an after dinner mint beside the cup, but you could use ramekins if you prefer and serve with ratafias or shortbread. You need a large crock pot to cook them.*

chocolate
pots

SERVES 6

450 ml/¾ pint/2 cups single (light) cream

2.5 ml/½ tsp vanilla essence (extract)

175 g/6 oz/1½ cups coarsely grated plain (semi-sweet) chocolate with 70% cocoa solids

25 g/1 oz/2 tbsp caster (superfine) sugar

2 large eggs

120 ml/4 fl oz/½ cup double (heavy) or whipping cream

15 ml/1 tbsp cocoa (unsweetened chocolate) powder

1 Put the single cream, vanilla essence and chocolate in a saucepan and heat gently, stirring, until the chocolate melts. Remove from the heat.

2 Whisk together the sugar and eggs, then whisk into the chocolate mixture. Spoon into six small cups or ramekins (custard cups).

3 Stand the cups in the crock pot with enough boiling water to come half way up the sides of the containers (if necessary, prop the middle dish up on the outside ones). Cover and cook on Low for 1½–2 hours until just set. Do not overcook. Remove from the crock pot, leave to cool, then chill.

4 Whip the double cream until peaking and spoon on top of each chilled pot of chocolate. Dust with sifted cocoa and serve.

Crème caramel or flan *is popular all over the Mediterranean. You can make it into a boozy dessert by substituting 45 ml/3 tbsp of the milk with brandy or a liqueur such as Tia Maria or Cointreau. Make individual ones or one large one, whichever you prefer – but if you cook small ones they will take only 2–3 hours to set.*

caramel
cream

SERVES 6

175 g/6 oz/¾ cup caster (superfine) sugar
600 ml/1 pint/2½ cups milk

4 eggs
1.5 ml/¼ tsp vanilla essence (extract)

1 Put 100 g/4 oz/½ cup of the sugar in a small heavy-based pan. Heat it gently until it dissolves, then boil rapidly for a few minutes until it turns a deep golden brown.

2 Immediately pour the caramel into the base of a 1 litre/1¾ pint/ 4¼ cup soufflé dish or pudding basin. Quickly swirl the dish so the caramel coats the base before it sets.

3 Whisk together the milk, eggs, vanilla essence and the remaining sugar. Strain into the soufflé dish, cover with foil and stand the dish in the crock pot. Add enough boiling water to come half way up the side of the dish. Cover and cook on Low for 4–5 hours until just set.

4 Leave to cool, then chill. Loosen the edge before turning out on to a serving dish.

Nocino is an Italian walnut liqueur traditionally made with green walnuts but you can make a delicious version in a slow cooker with ordinary shelled ones. It can be served with cheese instead of port. If you want to make half, or even a quarter, of this quantity, make it in a small slow cooker or in a dish in a large cooker with 5 mm/¼ in of boiling water in the crock pot.

walnut liqueur
with pears and ratafias

SERVES 4 FOR DESSERT, 15–20 AS A LIQUEUR

A 700 ml/scant 1¼ pint bottle of
   vodka
1 cinnamon stick
12 cloves
1 blade of mace
250 g/9 oz/generous 1 cup caster
   (superfine) sugar

100 g/4 oz/1 cup shelled walnuts

TO SERVE:
4 ripe pears
8–12 ratafias

1 Pour the vodka into the crock pot and add the spices and sugar. Wash the walnuts thoroughly in a colander, then roughly chop and add to the pot. Stir well to dissolve the sugar. Cover and cook on Low for 5 hours.

2 Remove the pot from the container and leave to cool.

3 Strain the liqueur through a fine mesh or piece of muslin (cheesecloth) and pour into the vodka bottle. Discard the spices, but the nuts can be used in a cake or dessert or sprinkled over fruit salad, if you like.

4 Screw the cap on the bottle and store the liqueur in a cool, dark place. It can be drunk straight away but if possible leave it for several months for the full flavour to develop and to allow the sediment to settle.

5 To serve as a dessert, peel, core, and dice the pears. Put a small pile on each of four small plates with the ratafias. Pour four small glasses of liqueur and stand one on each plate. Serve with small forks to spear the pear to dip into the liqueur with the ratafias.

INDEX